PEOPLE
WHO MAKE
YOUR LIFE
HELL

Managing the people
who try to control you

LOIS GRANT

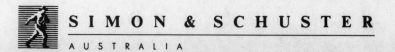

SIMON & SCHUSTER

AUSTRALIA

To my children: Marigail, Keltie, James and Robert, who
taught me the awesome responsibility of valuing difference,
and to Al Haggar, who thought it was all possible.

PEOPLE WHO MAKE YOUR LIFE HELL
First published in Australia in 2001 by
Simon & Schuster (Australia) Pty Limited
20 Barcoo Street, East Roseville NSW 2069

A Viacom Company
Sydney New York London Toronto Singapore

© Lois Grant 2001

National Library of Australia
Cataloguing-in-Publication data:

Grant, Lois
    People who make your life hell : managing the people who try to control
    you.

    ISBN 0 7318 1042 2

    1. Manipulative behaviour. I. Title.

158.2

Cover and internal design: Sue Rawkins
Typeset in Sabon 11 pt on 14 pt
Printed in Australia by Griffin Press on 79gsm Bulky Paperback

10 9 8 7 6 5 4 3 2

CONTENTS

Manipulation is a subtle and insidious form of abuse. If you allow a manipulator to sneak up on you, before you know it, you are overpowered.

No-one has the right to abuse you. If you are suffering from abuse, you need to be able to access the information you want as quickly as possible. The book has been designed for this purpose. Start with the Introduction because it will explain how to use the book. Then come back to this contents listing, find the description that fits the person who is making your life hell. Go straight to that chapter. Each chapter is self-contained – you'll find out what the manipulator is up to, how to stop their abuse and still give the relationship a chance.

If you have been managing your bully with counter-bullying strategies, you may find yourself in here! You can do better than that! This book will show you stronger ways to get what you want without feeling nasty or guilty.

THE CHESHIRE CAT. These are bullies who are cold, detached and destructive, projecting an illusion of superiority and ultimate intelligence. They play judge and jury but never contribute.
p. 37

MARY HAD A LITTLE LAMB. She's the bully who appears to be a friend, while orchestrating our feelings of inadequacy. She kills with kindness. She gains control by gently encouraging us not to trust our judgment, making us dependent on her.
p. 46

LITTLE JACK HORNER. His fear of being beaten or not being recognised for his achievements keeps him moving at full speed. It's hell when he loses. You need to stop his abuse but not his talent.
p. 55

SLEEPING BEAUTY. She is thrilled to see us – until a better offer comes along. Her identity is based upon being linked with very important people. She won't let anyone get close to her in case they see she is empty and fragile.
p. 66

THE LION AND THE UNICORN. These are bullies who are trying to eradicate each other. Never put yourself in the middle of a war. A good chapter for parents and managers.
p. 76

MARY, MARY, QUITE CONTRARY. She is noted for killing ideas, having a deep fear of making mistakes. Don't give up when she keeps saying 'It won't work'. Her obsession for detail can be very useful!
p. 87

THE GRAND OLD DUKE OF YORK. He bullies us by resisting change. He clings to the good old days and ways. We help him march forward – constructively!
p. 97

THE OLD WOMAN WHO LIVED IN A SHOE. She is a long-suffering martyr who has to do everything herself, yet if you attempt to help her you will meet with resistance, not gratitude.
p. 105

ROCK-A-BYE BABY. These victims of a negative environment may never leave their cradle. They are low in confidence and highly critical of themselves for their lack of success. They are terrified of making decisions or taking risks. We help them leave the cradle.
p. 115

LITTLE MISS MUFFET. She seems so helpless and incapable but is surprisingly powerful. She is afraid of failure so entangles the competent in her web to take responsibility for her life.
p. 127

LITTLE BO-PEEP. She will drain your energy by always expecting you to guess what her problem is, a task you'll never achieve. She also wants you to tell her what to do so that you will take responsibility if it doesn't work out.
p. 141

OLD MOTHER HUBBARD. She is dedicated to 'financial incompetence', lurching from one plastic card crisis to another. She never

INTRODUCTION

Every one of us has encountered a bully at some point in our life – someone who makes your life hell! Bullies come in various disguises: manipulating, humiliating or pretending you aren't worth their time. Maybe you've reacted to the abuse by counter-attacking and have worn the guilt for years. This is because you are a decent person, concerned about how you treat your fellow human beings. Or maybe you ran away from a bad situation and have been haunted by unfinished business.

Reacting by attacking or running for the hills works in the short term, but neither of these approaches can change the culture of 'Kill or be Killed' that puts us all at risk. Confronting a bully requires strength and courage, and the intelligence to offer him or her a chance to reform. You may need to begin with someone in your family or with a friend, and some bosses badly need direction. Whingeing in the washroom may feel satisfying, but it doesn't change what's going on.

I've selected real-life cases for use as examples of the many different kinds of bullying, drawn from my work as a lecturer in communication, counselling individuals, families, communities and the corporate world – at every level. These stories will give you the insight and the tools both to stop and change the relationship. They are designed to reinforce your skills, your courage and your confidence.

I've chosen fairy tale characters to help uncover the masks that manipulative bullies wear to try to control our lives. The characters are universal myths and I hope their use will lighten your burden and help you see through their disguise with greater clarity. For example, Mary Quite Contrary always says 'It can't be done', squashing incoming ideas. Old King Cole makes you laugh so much that you forget you are doing the work he said he would do. The Bear who attacks Algy is a cost-effective killer – publicly attacking one person in order to control the whole group. In each chapter I have referred to the chosen character by their gender, but trust me, men, women and children can all play the Queen of Hearts or Little Jack Horner if you let them. I'm a 'still-trying-to-reform-myself' Jack Horner, the unstoppable competitor. I'd appreciate your help in stopping me climbing up Mt Everest backwards!

At the end of each chapter, I give you a list of specific things to try. You need to trust your judgment, but rest assured that every time you try to stop the abuse, you will gain in skill and confidence. Bullies recognise this – there is no point in them continuing the abuse if it doesn't get them what they want.

Bullies are very empathetic. That's how they can sense your fear, shift gears and continually hone in on your most vulnerable place in order to control you. Bullies give empathy a bad name! You'll need to use compassion and toughness when dealing with your bully, and you'll learn a lot about keeping your own life intact. If you don't want to feel compassionate towards someone who is making your life hell, remember, we are all survivors in a very critical society. I've found that most bullies want to feel secure enough to stop playing dirty and find someone they can trust. You may not win them all but you may feel more confident in letting go of an unhealthy relationship. Two people have to be committed to building a relationship or it has no place to grow.

Lastly, I've changed the real names in the stories so you can't turn around and say 'Harry, your story's in the book!'.

HERE'S TO YOU MANAGING THE PEOPLE WHO MAKE YOUR LIFE HELL!

THE QUEEN OF HEARTS

*'No, no!' said the Queen. 'Sentence first, verdict
afterwards.'*
*'Stuff and nonsense!' said Alice loudly. 'The idea of
having the sentence first!'*
'Hold your tongue!' said the Queen, turning purple.
'I won't!' said Alice.
*'Off with her head!' the Queen shouted at the top of
her voice.*
Nobody moved.

LEWIS CARROLL, *ALICE'S ADVENTURES IN WONDERLAND*

The Queen of Hearts can change from calm to gale force
winds in one breath if she wants to be critical or doesn't get
her way. Her aim is to intimidate the opposition into instant
submission, and we are all the opposition! Never say to her,
'Let's be rational'. She doesn't intend to be – she is irrational to
put us off balance. She hopes everyone is listening when she
explodes – it's a cost-effective way of bringing you into submission. You are going to learn not to react or submit to her
bullying; instead, you are going to offer her a chance to trust –
and improve her relationship with – another human being.

Jane found a flat near the university in her first year. Another student in the building offered to give her a lift one morning, and Jane gratefully accepted.

Her gratitude was short-lived. The student marched into the flat, brushed Jane aside, and said, 'Haven't you unpacked these boxes yet? Are you proposing to use that chair as a wardrobe? There is a closet, you know. How are you going to manage university if you can't manage one room?'

Jane cringed at the tone of voice. She was humiliated and found herself on the defensive. She tried to explain that she had arrived only the day before, but the other woman cut her off. Her excuses were not good enough! Jane felt inadequate and exposed.

That day, Jane couldn't remember a word she heard in lectures; her mind kept going over and over the morning's interaction. She felt such a wimp for letting a complete stranger dictate to her and she had no idea what she had done to make it happen.

The Queen of Hearts likes to start off a relationship by creating a reign of terror, usually through a personal attack, hoping that you will be submissive or keep your distance. For her to feel safe, she needs to think that she is in control. She wants you to believe she is superior, yet she is very lonely.

The Queen of Hearts is deliberately irrational. She blows up in your face without warning, taking authority where she has none. She also carves you up with cutting criticism. It puts you off guard, and you cringe in disbelief as she ignores social expectations. Some people grovel, hoping for peace through submission, giving the Queen outrageous control. Bystanders laugh, partly because they don't know what else to do, but mostly because the attack is not aimed at them, while the victim shrinks with embarrassment.

The Queen would like you to believe that she is a brave, 'I don't care what people think' eccentric, but she cares very much what people think, for she is afraid you might find fault with her. Her surprise attack is intended to send you scurrying for cover. The Queen seeks a partner who is exceptionally kind, someone who will easily believe it's their fault for upsetting her. After the Queen gets her way, both she and her partner pretend the outburst never happened. She expects you to do the same. It's a hit-and-deny-it strategy, leaving you wondering if anything ever actually happened.

The Queen wants you to believe that she is the ultimate authority on everything. Her standards would scare God. But is she happy? No, she is deeply unhappy. She nurtures herself at the expense of others, but it doesn't make her happy. She has no confidence. She does nothing to gain it. She doesn't value the rights of others because she is too busy protecting herself from her perceived 'scary' world. Her partner usually runs around behind her, repairing the damage, saying that the Queen didn't really mean it. Of course she did! She doesn't want you to get close and sense her fear.

The word 'eccentric' is a kind of social dispensation, allowing the Queen to be outrageous and abusive. Meanwhile, she can sense your vulnerability and she goes for it. As she wraps herself in chains of insecurity, she wants you to pay for the chains.

The Queen can be particularly vicious to her family. Ask yourself: if you weren't related, would you choose to see her? The answer would probably be no. Keeping up the happy family image can hide a lot of pain. It doesn't hold the Queen accountable for the wake of destruction, and it doesn't help you learn to stop her abusive behaviour. Her protectors claim that she isn't always like this, allowing the Queen of Hearts to get away with it. However, you don't have to take such a passive position. You are going to stop her and give her a chance to come out from under her crown.

The Queen of Hearts lives perpetually in the past, reinforcing her belief that she has been deprived and treated unjustly. She may have been, but she lives in despair (of her own creation), instead of learning from her experiences with people and getting on with who she wants to be.

You can learn to protect yourself from the Queen's attacks. After the first encounter, expect more of the same. Lowering your eyes and pretending it isn't happening will only encourage her. If you're not afraid, can't be intimidated and don't react, she will stop. There is no point in her carrying on the attack. The focus is squarely on her and she feels foolish. Besides, rage takes a lot of energy. Learn to see her as a ferocious marshmallow. Sit calmly and look her directly in the eye while she rages and performs. The purpose is not to humiliate her, but to be totally unimpressed.

Simon tried to play it safe by not introducing his partner to his parents, and getting married with only a few close friends around. His parents raged when he told them. He stood there on his own, eyes downcast, and took the avalanche. Six months after their wedding, his parents were still pressing for an invitation to dinner. He dreaded the thought, but he didn't know how he could avoid it any longer. He tried to explain his parents' eccentricity to his wife Sally, but she laughed. Little did she know!

Simon was right to feel apprehensive. As his mother swept through the door, she barely acknowledged Sally. Her opening gambit was to test for dust as she passed the first table. His father supported his mother by criticising Simon and Sally's choice of house, location and condition, saying, 'Why didn't you ask our opinion, before you made this costly mistake?'

What had ever possessed him to believe that they might act differently now that he was married? He began to explain that they couldn't afford a palace. Simon always thought he could win their respect by spelling out the facts. It had never worked before, but he still tried to be rational. Simon got two sentences out before Sally sailed past him. Her cheery voice welcomed his parents as she agreed that there was a lot of work to do.

She said to his mother, 'Aren't you kind – think how long it would be before we could hire good help.' To his horror, Sally handed his mother a duster. 'I just love impeccable people who volunteer their labour,' she said. 'We can have drinks when you finish.'

Then Sally asked Simon's father to block out his weekends for the next six months and to remember to bring all his tools and equipment. 'We'll tell you exactly what you need to do!' she assured him. She meant it, and they knew she meant it. They ate and ran.

Sally had called Simon's parents' bluff. There was no way they would accept the responsibility. That might open them to another's critical appraisal. The Queen of Hearts believes her right is to judge your performance. Never defend yourself. Agree with her. She will be stumped if you look her in the eye and respond with gentle amusement:

Your desk is untidy. Yes, it is.
You waste a lot of time watching TV. Yes, I do.
These potatoes are overcooked. You're right.
That tie is terrible. Got it for 20 cents – everyone loves it!

A Queen can bully you only if you feel embarrassed. Humour, not used as a weapon, stops them cold.

Toby was showing visitors around his garden. One of them commented sarcastically that the weeds outnumbered the flowers. Toby smiled comfortably and said 'That's because I have tame weeds. I say "sit", and they don't move until I come to get them. It's wonderful to find someone who can tell a weed from a pansy. When can you come to help me?' Strangely enough, the person did.

You are accountable to no one but yourself. Nobody owns you. You don't have to feel pressured when someone makes a judgmental statement in a punitive voice.

Your newspaper is on the floor. So it is.

You have the right to leave your newspapers anywhere you like, except on someone else's floor or a shared floor. But that's a matter for negotiation.

Notice that the Queen leaves other bullies alone. If you don't submit to her, she is at a loss. The more she rages, the more comfortable you become. Listen quietly, with respect, while she rants, rehearsing what you are going to say when she runs out of breath. Calmness in the face of intimidation leaves her with nothing to say. Be unimpressed. Remain neutral.

The basic rule in dealing with any Queen of Hearts is, 'If you want my respect and cooperation, you'll have to earn it'. State this calmly, when she has run out of steam, then walk out quietly, withdrawing with dignity. Do not run – that encourages her. You may only withdraw to the next room, your bathtub, or you may go for a walk – whatever will nurture you at that moment.

Don't be surprised when you get back together if nothing is mentioned. That's fine. The Queen will give you more opportunities to smile and remind her of the rule: *If you want my respect and cooperation, you'll have to earn it.*

The Queen rants – you withdraw your cooperation. Give her nothing to fight against. Don't placate, don't make excuses, don't argue. Arguing is a sign of desperation and does not solve the problem. It produces resistance and is manipulative.

Never justify abuse. 'She's not always like this' or 'Don't get him upset'. The Queen of Hearts chooses to get upset. If she doesn't show a genuine improvement and doesn't communicate with emotional intelligence, why continue? Never forget: if neither people are committed to the relationship, there is no relationship. Your compassion will provide the patience while they learn but there should be evidence that they are committed to learning. Compassion for yourself mean you will never accept abuse.

There's no such thing as a little abuse. Respect does not abuse. If you allow a Queen to repress you, you are seen as soft, and easy prey. She feels a surge of power and you are punished for the pain, real or imagined, she feels inside.

If you fear physical threat, call the appropriate authorities, or go for help. Never hesitate. Use the neighbours only in cases of emergency. The neighbours want peace, and they may discount your fear. The Queen can be quick to make a liar of you, by calming down and looking good. You look like the one lacking in emotional control.

Tell the Queen of Hearts what the consequences of abuse will be. Never promise what you can't deliver, and never hesitate to deliver it. If the Queen isn't accountable for her abuse, why would she stop it?

The Queen can move from verbal to physical violence if her anger is unchecked and she loses emotional control:

Sarah ended up in hospital frequently, telling everyone she'd tripped. She never turned Roy in because she loved him and knew he would be devastated at what he'd done. He would beg her forgiveness. She wanted to believe him. She felt sorry for him losing control, and believed him when he said she provoked him, although he never said in what way. She was also afraid of making it on her own with two children.

Sarah was badly hurt but when she got home from hospital and Roy cuddled up beside her. They made tender love, and she thought she was safe at last. She thought Roy wouldn't hit her again, but he did. He became more vicious and she got closer to dying.

Compassion begins at home. In asking for mutual respect, and expecting to get it, you are defining the outcome you want, and laying the foundation for reciprocal respect. If trust develops and the Queen feels more secure, there is less need to chop off heads. Remember, what drives a Queen of Hearts is the fury of feeling inadequate and a need to control you through intimidation.

Charlotte and Edward celebrated their sixty-fifth wedding anniversary with a family gathering. Their children didn't think it was much of a celebration. Charlotte never stopped attacking Edward. He never stopped trying to comply. It was miserable for everybody. The children told their parents that they were not coming to another family gathering unless the couple underwent marriage counselling.

'Don't be ridiculous,' screamed Charlotte, the Queen of Hearts. 'Nothing could get him to act intelligently!'

Her family persisted. 'You are a terrible example to the

rest of the family. It's like descending into hell.' In the end, the elderly couple agreed.

The counsellor asked what they wanted to get out of the session. Charlotte spoke immediately. She wanted Edward to 'smarten up'. The counsellor then asked her husband what he wanted. He answered very simply: 'To die'.

Charlotte said, 'I told you he was stupid.'

The counsellor took him seriously. 'When?' she asked.

'I think next week,' he replied calmly. 'I'm tired of trying and never succeeding.'

His wife realised he was serious and began to sob. 'How could I live without you? I can't survive without you.'

That amazed him. 'You are the strong one, you don't need me. I've never done anything right. You've made that abundantly clear,' he said.

'I had to put you down,' she said. 'I'm ugly. You are handsome, intelligent, everybody loves you. I knew that if I didn't break your confidence, you'd leave me for somebody else.'

He looked at her in genuine surprise. 'I have always loved, admired and respected you,' he said sadly. 'I just wish I had been able to make you happy.'

'But you did, my darling. I have blessed every day that you stayed with me. It was a miracle that you could even like me. I was so afraid of losing you.' The counsellor slipped away discreetly.

Be compassionate enough to stop the Queen of Hearts. Know that inside, she is suffering a great deal.

The local hospital was running workshops for parents with teenage children. Adolescent separation can be a traumatic time, even in the best of families. The teenagers know that discovering who they are is a journey they have to make alone, even if they are living at home. Many of them only know how to do it rebelliously. There were 20 people at the hospital workshop one morning. When Sophie, a 14-year-old, was asked what she wanted out of the workshop, her mother Helen answered for her, 'We're here because Sophie's hopeless.' Sophie shrank.

'Hopeless at what?' the counsellor asked.

'Everything,' was her mother's reply.

The counsellor recounted several things he saw Sophie do well. The mother discounted them. 'Anybody can do that. She's stupid at school.'

Sophie straightened up. 'I'm good at school,' she said with a bit of spirit.

'Did you hear that?' shrieked her mother. 'Rebellious!' The group twitched uncomfortably.

'But Mother, I *am* good at school,' Sophie said.

Her mother doubled the shriek. 'Not at English and maths, you're not! You're a write-off!'

It turned out that Sophie got 90 per cent in maths, 95 per cent in English and top marks in her other subjects. The entire group was ready to lynch Helen.

A bit of exploration disclosed the Helen's background. She had been sexually abused from the age of three by her father and two uncles. When she turned to her mother for help, she was told to 'Shut up. You've got a roof over your head.'

When she was eleven, Helen ran away from home and supported herself in the only way she knew how – prostitution. She married a drunk, like her father, and was bringing up her daughter alone.

When asked why she wanted her daughter to get 100 per cent in every subject, the woman stared in disbelief. 'Do you think I want her to be like me? I want her to have a chance!'

The counsellor asked Helen who she thought she sounded like when she spoke to her daughter. Helen looked as if she'd been struck. She whispered, 'My mother'.

The group sat in compassionate silence.

The counsellor said softly, 'You can choose to mother yourself. You deserve a lot of love.' Helen wept, and everyone tried to hold her – they wanted to hug away her pain.

TAKE YOUR HEAD OFF THE CHOPPING BLOCK

• When she meets with opposition, the Queen of Hearts launches an attack to cover her doubt and vulnerability.

• The best way to deal with the Queen of Hearts is to show that you are not afraid of her tirade of abuse.

• Do not be submissive. Listen to her rant, but remain neutral and look her in the eye. Walk away if her abuse goes over the top.

• Call her bluff and agree with her, but exaggerate her criticism using gentle humour.

• Tell her she has to earn your respect or you won't cooperate, then withdraw with dignity. Expect her never to mention the incident when she returns but expect better behaviour, too. If she blows up, stick by your rules. Remember, she may need lots of chances.

• Never placate, never make excuses and never argue with a Queen of Hearts.

• Never justify her behaviour.

• Be compassionate. She needs it.

• Don't confuse compassion with patronising behaviour. Compassion is the ability to believe we can help each other in a very critical society. Bullies need compassion *and* limits.

ALGY MET A BEAR

(AND WAS PROMPTLY CONSUMED)

Algy met a bear,
The bear met Algy.
The bear was bulgy,
'cause the bulge was Algy.

The Bear tries to control you by pretending he is a ferocious bear the minute you express an opinion that doesn't suit him. He chews you up.

You'll encounter the Bear in all shapes and sizes. He may reside in the schoolyard; ridiculing another child, getting other children to join him. Many children feel safer from victimisation if they join the Bear, but they are never safe. It takes enormous courage to stand up to him.

> It was the annual school camp. There were noisy kids who were mingling happily everywhere. That's why nobody could believe what happened. A small boy named Henry hurled a rock at a bigger child. The rock struck John in the temple and he died a few hours later.
>
> At the investigation, parents tried to shield their children from the trauma. They said it was just an accident, a rare moment when a child lost control for no reason at all. Everyone agreed. Their statements said there was no evidence of animosity, except that Henry seemed to play alone. Henry refused to speak. 'Weirdo' was the verdict, and everyone blamed Henry's parents.

Suddenly a child stood up and asked to speak. He was shaking and his parents tried to hold him back. 'I have to speak. We all know why it happened!' He looked around at his classmates. 'Why don't you tell them?' The tears rolled down his face. Everyone tried to silence him: 'It's happened!' 'It's an accident!' 'There is no point in dragging it on!' 'It's a tragedy!'

But the child kept on. 'We picked on him. We hounded him every day at school. It was fun because he ran. We chased him, we pushed him, we called him gutless. Anyone who tried to stay out of it had to choose Henry or us.'

'We found Henry trying to hide his sleeping bag. You could smell it – he'd wet his bed. John grabbed it, and held it up for everyone to see and smell. We all shrieked with laughter and held our noses. Henry tried to grab it back, but John ran outside with it, calling for everyone to come and smell. That's when the rock hit John.'

There was a stunned silence as he sat down. The room exploded with indignant voices and the child heard a whisper in his ear, 'Now you'll get yours'. A new bully had moved into the void.

The Bear has a desperate need to mask his inadequacy; intimidating others gives him an illusion of power and helps hide the pain within him. You are going to stop the Bear and give him a choice: does he want you to cooperate and support him in helping to stop his behaviour or would he prefer to lose a friend?

Your first encounter with the Bear is intended to surprise and confuse you, to put you off balance. You become rattled, while the Bear pretends it's funny that you are stupid because you don't 'get it'.

You are not stupid. There is no way you own the information in another person's head. You are not wrong, either, but the Bear will pass judgment on what you say or think as if he is both judge and jury. Don't accept that judgment. The Bear is, in effect, asking you to change your viewpoint to accommodate his needs. If he demands that you change because you are stupid or wrong, and he is not considering your needs, it is an act of injustice.

The Bear picks on vulnerable people to give himself a sense of power, an illusion of strength. If you are low in confidence, shy, or eager to please, the Bear will smell your vulnerability. He sees kindness as weakness; he is not used to being cared for, he is used to being hurt.

The Bear thrives on anger, arrogance, superiority and a belief that he has the right to punish the world for what the world has done to him. He is locked in the belief that other people are his enemy and he has the right to crush them. The Bear needs to learn to trust.

So how do you protect yourself when encountered by the Bear? You don't react. By reacting, you are allowing your fear to smother your logic. You need your brain to be functioning at its best, both logically and emotionally, to stop the Bear. You need skills of toughness to stop the first attack, combined with compassion, patience and sensitivity. Why sensitivity? Well, the pain in the Bear is deep-seated. He has built a concrete shelter around his feelings so that he won't feel pain. Yet *your* feelings are your radar, your source of creativity, your genius, your self.

The Bear isn't born a bully. He learns how to bully from somebody who is bullying him. The Bear is a courageous survivor who knows no other way. Like any bully, he seeks a sense of safety by victimising the rest of us. You may not feel like being his friend, but the Bear needs a friend he can trust, a friend who won't be impressed by his attempts to intimidate others.

You can learn to do that by stopping the Bear's abuse, calmly and with respect, while offering him support in return for mutual respect. You must learn to have the personal courage and integrity to ask, 'How can I help you?' but only after he's simmered down.

What the Bear needs is what we all need most: support, acceptance, recognition and safety. You can offer him that. You won't change him overnight, but once the Bear learns to trust and give mutual respect, our community is a safer place because the Bear is no longer out for revenge. A reformed Bear is good at helping other Bears take a risk to trust.

Sarah was doing a tour through a juvenile remand centre when she heard a roar of angry voices. As she rounded the corner, Sarah saw three bigger boys victimising a smaller boy of about ten. The boy was missing all his front teeth. He was trying to hold a painting of a road and mountains out of the reach of his tormentors.

The older boys were ridiculing him. 'Purple mountains? You idiot!'

Sarah moved between them. Facing the older boys she said quietly, 'Have you ever lived in mountains?'

'No,' they said sheepishly.

'Well I have,' she smiled at them. Turning to the artist she looked at his painting and was surprised. His perspective was good: the colours and size of the mountains faded into the distance beside a winding road.

Sarah said to him, 'It's beautiful. That's just the way it looks in the evening. It's almost as if you've been there.'

She had walked down the corridor when the child caught up with her. 'I would like you to have this,' he said. He looked gratefully into her eyes and gave her the painting. She framed it and hung it in her bedroom. It was the first thing she saw every morning – it was the road to freedom. She wondered if he had discovered how to walk it.

Be aware that not every Bear roars at first. Some start by punishing slowly, using humour as a serrated knife, humiliating or ridiculing you. They watch you boil or bleed, feigning surprise when you 'can't take a joke'. Personal attack is never a joke. Discounting what anyone says or believes is never a joke. Highlighting mistakes you make, or things you forget, is never a joke. It is brutality; it is verbal abuse and if you allow it, the Bear will keep intensifying his brutality, taking as much as you let him control.

The Bear can shift ground very quickly if he senses he's gone too far. He will ask your forgiveness in between bouts of verbal abuse, and promise to change. You want to believe him because you are living in hope that the agony will end. It may, but you need to see evidence that what he says is what he is doing. If not, withhold cooperation - he hasn't earned it!

The Bear manipulates you through your guilt. He wants you to believe that he was born this way, and that you have no right to change his personality. He will say that you made him angry because you didn't meet his needs. He expects you to guess what he wants. That puts you in an impossible position; you can't guess what's in anybody's head so a temper tantrum is his choice. He chooses to lose control and to victimise you. Each time you allow yourself to be victimised, you lose confidence, and encourage brutality. You need the skills and confidence to stop him.

You may tell yourself that you're not going to put up with it any more, but if you've opted for peace by accepting the responsibility of guessing what makes him angry, he's trapped you. You may have done this because you are so low in confidence, you can't think straight, and perhaps afraid to be alone. It's easy to weaken your power by thinking: where would I go? What could I do? You could have become so exhausted that you can't see that the door to freedom and self-control is always open. There are always options: if the bully left you, you'd be forced to make decisions to take control of your life.

As manipulation is deliberately irrational, don't try to make sense out of a temper tantrum. Also note how selective bullies are in their choice of victim. A bully may be perfectly rational in the company of others, then brutalise you in private. If other people never see or hear the bully's acts of brutality towards you, you may appear to be the one who is emotionally unstable if you try and share your problem with them. Bullies use this double standard to advantage, as proof that it is *you* who is setting them off. It's easy for you to doubt who you really are!

The Bear can intimidate his way to the top in organisations if others are compliant and see intimidation as strong leadership. That's the myth of an aggressive culture. Once we are compliant we expect a leader to protect us! Real leaders develop leaders. They believe their job is to identify and maximise the potential of every employee, bringing out their leadership potential. Real leaders want to work with, not compete with strong people. Bullies who pretend they are leaders say the right things, such as 'Our people are our greatest resource', or 'We want your ideas', but they don't mean it. Just suggest an idea and see how quickly both you and the idea are squashed. If you are good at your job, the bully will feel threatened. The Bear chooses bright people to make him look good, then tells the world how inadequate they are.

Learn to stop a bully. Practise it! Look them calmly in the eye. The more relaxed and confident you are, the safer you are. Confident people can see past the growl and into the vulnerability of an abuser. They don't fold or run. One person's inquisitive and compassionate response to an emotional explosion was, 'Do you usually try to scare people? It must be hard on your health.' The bully regained control instantly.

In a meeting an abusive manager was calmly asked by a new employee why he tried to intimidate others. The bully turned to his staff and roared, 'I'm not intimidating, am I?'

His staff smiled anxiously and said, 'Oh, we've got used to him. He's okay once you get to know him.'

The manager smirked benignly at the person who'd asked the question. The smile faded when that person asked, 'Will I have to get used to something I don't like?' That was when everybody learned to get on with their jobs and keep the manager informed so he didn't have reason to rant and rave. He felt more secure. The staff managed their manager constructively and got on with developing their career skills. It began when someone had the courage to explore the expectations without attacking or complying with the demands of the abusive manager.

Sometimes the Bear chooses to be irrational in public to impress upon others how important he is.

A bully's flight was cancelled. In an airport lounge filled with people whose flights had also been cancelled, he proclaimed his importance by abusing the staff. The manager of the lounge smiled comfortably, 'How can I help you if you terrify me to death?'

The people nearby who heard her laughed. To save his embarrassment, she quickly whisked him behind a closed door where he was told that if he asked nicely, she would do

her best to get him to his destination with a minimum of fuss.
The Bear took one look at her calm, direct eyes and listened.

Being happy and in control of your life is your responsibility. If
you take on the job of making others happy, you give them permission to hold you responsible for their choices. This can
produce anger and emotional violence.

Abusive behaviour is never okay! Never condone, accept or
be impressed by abuse. Respect and trust are inseparable gifts
and you deserve them. There are many ways in which you can
train yourself to handle ferocious Bears, and you can ask trusted
friends to help you.

Clara was finishing her degree in Social Science. She was a
deeply committed Christian who felt that her calling was to
work with juveniles in detention centres.

Rob, her tutor, was worried about her. She was offended
whenever anyone said 'Darn'. Rob had worked in a detention
centre and knew that the juveniles would attack her with the
vilest language they could dispense, the moment they recognised how vulnerable she was.

The tutorial class was learning how to interview a juvenile
pending a court appearance. Clara was playing the role of
the professional. Rob chose to play the alleged offender.
Clara asked his name. His response was 'F*** off'.

Nobody moved. Clara began to tremble. The tremble
became deep, wrenching sobs. Rob reached out and took her
hands in his. 'Did you think I would let you go out there, so
committed and so vulnerable?'

'But that's where I want to contribute,' she sobbed.

'And you can,' he said, 'providing you realise they are
using that language to frighten you. They are scared and

they don't trust you. You are the enemy. If you don't react, their words have no effect. There is no point in them using them. You can get through to them faster if you treat them calmly, with warmth, respect and confidence, no matter what they say. You can be caring and capable of setting limits at the same time.'

Clara looked at Rob for a long time, then said 'Help me'.

It was a strange tutorial. Clara sat in the centre and her classmates formed a tight circle around her. Clara was to smile and be gently amused at their choice of expletives, no matter what they said. She was to keep eye contact with whoever spoke. Each person in turn dished out every vile expression they could muster. It only ran three rounds. The taunters had run out of expletives. Clara moved from quivering distress to open, genuine laughter.

Clara had a remarkable career helping juveniles make survival choices. The crudest invitation was met with brilliant, gentle humour and unwavering respect. She was delightfully unshockable and never lost her self-respect. She helped children at risk to develop theirs.

You can't change others, but you can change yourself. Lightly and calmly, choose to create the responses you want. Confident people respect themselves, and they treat others with equal respect. They don't have to fight or run. Confidence will enable you to choose not to endure any abuse, and you will be in a position to offer the Bear your help (if he asks nicely). Tell him the choices you are offering: support or withdrawal. If the Bear starts to roar, it is best to walk away calmly and not look back. Find a more valuable way to spend your time.

Is the Bear capable of change? Note how he calms down after he gets what he wants. Accept that abuse is the weapon of the very vulnerable. You are not going to fight, blame, argue, run away, or discuss the past. Your cooperation is available when you are treated with respect. You must believe in your right to live by those rules or you will never get them! If the Bear isn't interested in peaceful coexistence ask yourself, 'Why am I here?'

If threatened by physical abuse, don't hesitate to call in the authorities and press charges. There is to be no second chance. The bully must know the penalty for abusing you. You will need the courage to deliver! With abusive relationships, domestic violence and road rage on the increase, most communities offer anger management programs. If your bully is not willing to help himself, get help for yourself from community resources.

What reaction can you expect from the Bear when you do this? A massive attempt at intimidation, followed by 'I'll never do it again'. See that he doesn't!

If you don't follow through, the Bear will see you as weak. He feels weak and his weakness lies behind his intimidation. Weakness is something to destroy, and to do this, the Bear feels safer attacking anyone who is willing to take the abuse.

> Luke and Alice had separated many times. Luke was a violent drunk. The last separation came after Alice ended up in hospital. She told the doctors and nurses that she had fallen. Luke arrived with flowers, went down on his knees and begged forgiveness. The children were crying, begging her to give him a chance. Alice thought the agony was over. She awoke in the morning to see him looking down at her. His eyes were venomous. He said, 'You're so easy'. Those words set her free.

This is a dramatic example of how giving a Bear an inch can have serious consequences. You must stop abuse with the first put-down.

Father was a Grizzly Bear. Mother spent her time trying to guess what he wanted. When she asked him what he wanted he replied, 'If you weren't so stupid, you would know!'

Tragically, she submitted. She didn't realise that the next step was to say happily, 'When you tell me what you want, I'll be glad to help.'

The boys in the family thought it was a good system and they used the same tactics as their father. Why not? It seemed to work! They felt like very powerful men.

One of the boys, Jeremy, was an outstanding student and sportsman. It was assumed that he would end up with an impressive woman as his partner. Women flocked to him, hoping to be his chosen, each slavishly following fashion trends.

The day Jeremy arrived unexpectedly with his new wife, Jenny, the household was thrown into chaos. His mother took to her bed for three weeks. Jenny wore no make-up and wore thick glasses instead of contact lenses. She had no fashion sense. Everyone said, 'What does he see in her?'

It wasn't long before Jenny's husband reverted to his Bear routine. His mother rose from her bed, and her daughters rushed to her aid. Out of the kitchen came the bride. Jenny sauntered in casually in front of the roaring Bear without appearing to hear him.

The women exchanged glances – was she totally deaf? Jenny seemed to be looking for something. The roaring stopped and everyone stared. She finally noticed her husband. Looking him in the eye she asked, 'Have you seen my keys?'

In a perfectly normal tone of voice he said, 'I think they are on the table in the hallway.'

'Thanks,' she said and headed for the door.

She paused to smile at him and said, 'Enjoy your temper

tantrum, darling, then, if you want my support, ask me. I'll be in the kitchen.'

The mother and daughters stared in disbelief. Her husband stopped yelling and calmly followed Jenny to the kitchen.

This incredible woman never appeared on the cover of a woman's magazine, but a bronze statue of her should have been placed in a prominent position with a brass plaque proclaiming 'Bear Tamer'. Jenny knew who she was. She walked her own path with clarity and self-respect, and she taught a lot of women how to create respect for themselves. As she said, 'Charity begins at home'.

STOP THE ROAR, CLIP THE CLAWS – THEN LOVE THE BEAR

- The Bear likes to intimidate, humiliate and ridicule in public.
- Respond with toughness, compassion, patience, sensitivity and a strong 'STOP' sign.
- The Bear needs support, acceptance, recognition and safety.
- You both deserve respect and trust. Teach the Bear that your cooperation comes only with his respect for you.
- Don't try to justify or make sense of a tantrum – it is a deliberate manipulation.
- Learn to be relaxed and confident, and to look the Bear in the eye. Remember that abuse is the weapon of the vulnerable.
- Never condone or accept verbal abuse, especially when it comes wrapped up as a joke.
- Be consistent in stopping Bears.
- If you fear for your physical safety, press charges and don't cave in.
- You deserve to be loved and respected for yourself. It starts with you.

LITTLE GIRL WITH
A LITTLE CURL

(SHE WRAPS YOU AROUND HER CURL

AND GOES 'SQUISH')

There was a little girl, and she had a little curl
Right in the middle of her forehead.
When she was good she was very, very good,
But when she was bad, she was horrid.

The Little Girl with the Curl is like a hippopotamus whose beautiful eyes break the surface of the water. You have no idea of the force lurking below. In the name of survival, you have to learn how to manage the killing machine just below the surface. She is a charming person who holds centre stage effortlessly, is quick-witted and delightfully original but highly threatened if you don't comply. She is afraid of closeness but this is what she needs most – someone who won't be impressed by her temper, who can walk away shrugging their shoulders while loving the fragile person inside.

Alexandra was adorable when she was born. She gurgled her way into everybody's heart. As she grew older it was the same. She was great company, a joy to be with, until she didn't get what she wanted. She didn't waste time with charm when she was thwarted; she went ballistic. It was such a shock that this delightful person could suddenly produce a rage that was terrifying. Her helpless parents gave in, and the sun shone once more. Amazing. In a quest for peace, Alexandra's parents were so relieved that they colluded with her bullying behaviour. They never thought to develop a rule in their home that tempers are not rewarded and that there would be a consequence for being abusive such as time out from the family until she regained control, apologised and asked respectfully for what she wanted. As a result, Alexandra didn't develop the emotional discipline that she would badly need if she were to succeed in any area of her life.

She progressed through life, surrounded by adoring fans, none of whom dared to step out of line. 'She's a great person to be with,' they said, 'but don't get her upset. She goes off the rails.' Everyone adjusted their needs to suit hers. That is, until the day of her brother's wedding.

At the reception, someone who didn't know Alexandra's rules calmly disagreed with her. The roar shattered glasses in a 360-degree radius! The guests turned swiftly, took in the situation and wondered what Jack could have done to put her in this dreadful state. Jack, who had been attempting to state his point of view, stared at her with calm amusement. He didn't flinch, he didn't move, he didn't speak. He looked at her gently, without wavering.

Eventually, she ran out of steam. He was heard to say to her casually, 'I guess your family never learned to banish you when you tried this stuff as a kid. What a waste!' He smiled gently, then turned his attention to someone else as if the event had not occurred.

Alexandra stood there stunned. Jack had dismissed her as casually as if he were turning pages in a magazine. For the first time in her life, she didn't know what to do. She was furious and frightened. She also thought he was very attractive.

The Little Girl is the manipulator who offers so much more than temper tantrums. She has excellent social skills; she is a brilliant communicator who can walk into any environment and make it dance in the palm of her hand. She has the skills that diplomats would kill for. She is perfectly at home with anyone – she can defuse an icy atmosphere, and appraise other people's abilities in a few moments, unless your needs or viewpoints conflict with hers. Like a bolt of lightning in a clear blue sky, she attacks. It only takes a minute. It's so inappropriate that you can be thrown off balance, never questioning what right she has to abuse and demand, and you give in without thinking. That's why she does it. When she gets what she wants, it's all sunshine and flowers. She doesn't care where she is or who is watching. An audience's reaction is 'Who hurt her?' Its rational response is that someone must have done something dreadful to make anyone respond with such rage. But it's deliberately irrational. She is doing it to take control, and to get what she wants.

The result of this behaviour may be confusion. You can't think what you did to cause the eruption. Highly embarrassed, you withdraw, leaving her centre stage amidst nurturing fans. You look like the bully. After a few interactions like this, you choose your words carefully so as not to upset her.

The Little Girl is hell on her partner – she is a black widow spider who kills to control. Her partner becomes a compliant slave. In the hope of peace, he takes responsibility for the relationship, trying to guess what mood she'll be in and anticipating what might be wanted. Some partners are punished for asking if they can do anything. They get whacked with a 'You should know!' tantrum.

This manipulation, like any other, only works if you feel intimidated, embarrassed or at fault for causing the upset. You are especially vulnerable if you are a decent person committed to protecting others and making them happy. Manipulators don't attack confident people. They may get away with it once, but not a second time. Confident people analyse what has happened and create strategies for managing it next time – because there is always a next time.

There is injustice on both sides. For the victim, the injustice is not only the verbal abuse they receive, but the compassion of people who rush to rescue the attacker when she doesn't need helping at all. The victims are left with a sense of powerlessness, the pain of the abuse, and confusion. If you are closely connected by family or work to the Little Girl, you may even convince yourself that you are used to it.

For the Little Girl, the injustice is that she can never know if people really care for her or if they comply out of fear or obligation. Little Girls live in a very lonely place.

If you back off and avert your eyes, the attacker knows you have yielded, so she switches back to being adorable. The victim may try to clarify what happened, seeking justice, only to find that observers close in to protect the attacker without even knowing the facts. The victim is the one who is isolated and labelled a bully, while still wondering what happened.

If you opt for peace, you are, in a way, selling your soul. There is no way that your needs in the relationship will be considered if they conflict with those of the manipulator. If the Little Girl gets what she wants by attacking, why would she change? Unless you learn to set limits without fighting, you can look forward to a lifetime of all give but no get. As when handling any manipulation, if you want the relationship to last, you need to develop the skills to stop the attack without firing a shot. If you fail to implement these skills, the relationship won't last. You will feel powerless, you will feel you have failed, and you will carry guilt with you. In taking responsibility for the relationship, you accept a major injustice. If you walk away, the public is quick to blame you for the break-up. The Little Girl encourages this. What she needs to learn is that by reaching more balanced solutions, she will find greater confidence and security. A relationship is built on trust. One-way justice never works.

When she is abandoned by her partner, the Little Girl looks for an immediate replacement. The end of a relationship has her searching for someone to depend on – and even greater control. The combination of her being adorable and helpless is irresistible for those who are of a loving nature, and who see their role in life as protector and rescuer of the helpless. That doesn't help a Little Girl, who believes she must attack to stay in control. The protector and rescuer is constantly frustrated, and as a result, loses confidence and leaves, if he's lucky.

The Little Girl is good at playing at intimacy while not being interested in others at all. She doesn't love herself, so how can she love anyone else? If she risked loving you, she believes it would give you too much power over her. She merely exists; she is afraid of being alone and of silence because if she is alone and has to deal with something by herself, she is terrified. She needs the presence of a strong support system dedicated to her. For her, silence is a black void from which she might never return. Why? Whether the Little Girl shaves or applies make-up, she is still three years old, longing for what she destroys – a trusting relationship.

Separateness creates insecurity, so a relationship with her makes excessive demands on you. You will be asked to sacrifice the time you need to help yourself grow. You will become a permanent caretaker to someone demanding your full attention, protection and compliance, and an over-compliant partner is exceptionally boring to someone with social flair. Neither of you will discover who you are or could be. Living a life of such heavy responsibility can sap the life out of you. A healthy relationship feels comfortable, with each person taking time for themselves.

That's why Jack was so powerful at the wedding. He didn't lower his eyes, he didn't attack and he wasn't embarrassed. He looked at her with compassion. Alexandra needed to be rescued. In trying to get him to either fight or yield, bystanders had time to assess the situation – she was trying to victimise him.

It was Jack's compassion that cut so deeply into her facade. He dared to pity this star, this adorable creature. He wasn't afraid. He could see her manipulation for what it was, and he didn't feel threatened. In fact, Jack really lost interest. That really destroyed Alexandra. She was used to always being the centre of her world, surrounded by adoring protectors. Jack left her exposed for what she was – a predator!

Alexandra was stunned that Jack wasn't intimidated by her behaviour. He stood and listened in comfortable silence to her tirade. She felt totally exposed because he knew her temper tantrum was an act to get her own way. But what astounded her more was his compassion. She suddenly realised that nobody had known enough, or cared enough, to stop her in the past. She knew that others gave in, not because they cared, but because they didn't know what else to do. To let her get away with her abusive attacks was to sentence her to life as an obnoxious brat. No matter how much sun she produced, it couldn't melt the fear inside her. It was as if Jack could smell her fear of being left alone without the skills she needed to change. Deep in her heart Alexandra knew that people would associate with her but they would never like, admire, respect or trust her. They would enjoy her good side but ridicule her bad side in private.

Jack was a shattering experience for her. For the first time, Alexandra realised that she had no real relationships. No one with whom she could talk if she felt scared. She had never acknowledged how much her fear controlled who she was and how she acted.

The experience led Alexandra to do a very unusual thing. She opted for courage. She took the risk to find Jack. Would he hang up on her? Would he treat her with disdain? Would he ridicule her? She knew that she would feel embarrassed if she played cute and that he would be bored by it.

Jack had surprised her with his directness, his honesty. 'Have you been pulling the world around by the tail with this temper tantrum performance since you were a kid?' he had asked. It was genuine interest. Nobody had shown real interest in her before.

That's how the relationship began. Jack let the relationship build slowly, while Alexandra learned that negotiation was creating solutions so that both of them were happy. When she fell back into the old bad habits, Jack would smile and ask, 'What is it you want? Just ask and we'll work it out.'

Alexandra learned to negotiate calmly, quietly and intelligently. She was growing up.

Little Girls are not stupid. They can sense very quickly when you are not impressed or intimidated and it's a very powerful way of stopping them. See through the manipulation – all you have is a very frightened person trying to intimidate you into submission. *You* can choose not to be impressed. *She* must choose to stop the abuse. You cannot force her, but you can stop a Little Girl using you – you can leave.

If you suspect that the Little Girl's temper could turn into harmful behaviour towards herself or you, seek professional help. Don't wait for the hollow promises that automatically follow a violent interaction – act immediately.

The two *worst* things you can do when dealing with a Little Girl are:

• Tell her to calm down. She doesn't want to be calm, and by suggesting it you might incite a genuine loss of emotional stability. Listen to her with interest and respect. It's not a time for arrogance.

• You are not responsible for making her happy or unhappy – that's her job.

You are responsible for your own happiness and choices, as is she for hers. Put the responsibility back where it belongs – on her!

The two *best* things you can do are:

• Steep yourself in tranquillity whenever you have to listen to her in panic mode. Don't talk, just listen. You are not responsible for her losing control, even if she tells you that you are. She says you are to blame only to make you buckle under.

• Work out what she wants. Don't guess, ask her. If she's not willing to make a direct request, ask her to call when she's worked it out and wants cooperation. However, cooperation is not tax-free. You offer it on the condition of reciprocal respect.

Leave her in no doubt that the choice is up to her, and that the offer is open. If she doesn't call, you both know who made the choice. Never put up with abuse. Tell her to stop and call you when she is ready to resolve the issue. You may have to give the Little Girl many chances, as her commitment to total self-indulgence is deeply ingrained. It's her protection. It's up to her when she is ready to recognise that a good friend is waiting.

Don't think this form of manipulation is used by women only; men use it as a weapon as well.

Julia told her students that she expected excellent work in their assignments. She said that if she suspected poor work was a result of lack of interest or of not taking responsibility to ask for help if they needed it, she would assume they were wasting the taxpayer's time and money. She would give them a mark that would match their level of commitment.

One charmer didn't believe Julia. Philip always got his way. He was used to doing the very minimum that was necessary as he dazzled his way through life. He handed in a paper that he'd written at traffic lights. Julia gave him a big red zero, followed by a written invitation: 'If you decide to become academically enthusiastic, Philip, I'll be glad to help.'

He was not worried. He knew how to get what he wanted. He burst into Julia's office, threw the paper onto her desk, and strode around the room shouting obscenities that could be heard above the heavy traffic passing her window.

Julia sat calmly listening to his ranting, making no move to intervene. Philip had started so high in volume that he hadn't any room in which to manoeuvre, so he had to stop. Eventually. When he fell silent, Julia picked up his paper by the corner as if it were a dead rat.

'Are you asking me to accept this paper as an example of your intellectual capabilities?'

Philip wasn't stupid. He could see that he had two options. If he said 'yes', he suspected she would tell him the course was beyond his intelligence. That would wound his ego deeply, so he opted for the second possibility: a range of excuses. He thought of telling her that his brother had measles, but he hadn't heard of a case of measles that lasted for three months. Julia didn't respond to any of his excuses. He doubted if she had listened, although he thought they were pretty creative.

Instead Julia said, 'Would you like the opportunity to resubmit the paper?'

Philip relaxed. He was off the hook!

Until she said, 'You have exactly two days to resubmit. The paper will be in by 12 noon, not 12:01! It will be brilliant, and the most you can get is 45 per cent. It's up to you, 45 or zero.' She smiled comfortably, as if she'd asked him to a party. She hadn't been fazed by his temper tantrum or moved to pity by his excuses. She remained comfortably focused on the problem at hand.

Julia left the decision to him, content to accept whatever he decided. He stared at her. How could she be so tranquil in the face of his intimidation? She thanked him for coming and returned to her work. It was as if he didn't exist.

Philip was forced to decide. Did he want the degree or not? Hers was a core subject, and she wasn't going to influence him, one way or another. He couldn't remember going to bed at all. Forty-eight hours of panic and perspiration! She gave him 40 per cent.

Many years later, when Philip had achieved significance in his field, he asked her to lunch. She walked into his spacious office and noticed that her invitation to academic enthusiasm was beautifully framed behind his desk.

'Thank you for helping me grow up,' he said.

STABILISING LITTLE GIRLS WITH TEMPERS

• The Little Girl appears to be sweet and compliant, but she will hold you responsible for her unhappiness if she doesn't get her own way.

• She is afraid of being alone and of silence. If you help her to take responsibility for overcoming these fears by not being intimidated, you will also help her have adult relationships.

• Never try to calm down a Little Girl in tantrum mode, as this could incite genuine anger and real loss of control.
• Listen impassively to the tantrum. It's interactive TV in which you don't participate.
• You are not responsible for another person's happiness or unhappiness. The Little Girl has to make her own choices.
• You are not responsible for the Little Girl's loss of control.
• Ask her what it is that she wants and, if she is prepared to tell you, then you can work on resolving the issues together. You're giving her a chance to risk growing up and learning that life is a series of healthy, constructive, creative negotiations.

THE CHESHIRE CAT

A FRAGILE LITTLE KITTY DRESSED IN AN
ILLUSION OF SUPERIORITY

*'Well then,' the cat went on, 'You see a dog growls
When it's angry, and wags its tail when it's pleased.
Now I growl when I'm pleased
And I wag my tail when I'm angry.'*
THE CHESHIRE CAT, FROM LEWIS CARROLL'S *ALICE'S ADVENTURES
IN WONDERLAND*

Obscurity is the shield of the Cheshire Cat. Talking in riddles is an attempt to make you feel stupid, illiterate and inadequate. Cheshire Cats are mummified, hiding behind a mask of intellectual superiority. They are cold, detached and terrified that you might discover that they feel very inadequate. When you feel intimidated by them, you need to notice that they do very little. They read a little about a lot, but they rarely do anything except spout knowledge. They don't take risks because there is a chance of failure. Cats are pure theory. Without experience, they can never learn. They sit in a pool of knowledge yet don't know how to swim. They seek safety from exposure by watching you with disdain. They play judge and jury but don't contribute. You are going to use their broad knowledge and put a stop to their intimidation. There is no point in victimising you if you refuse to be a victim.

Every time they were invited out, Anna had to be inspected. George circled around her like a shark. If there was a tiny scuff on her shoe, he was livid. Whatever she wore was inadequate. She phoned around to see what the norm was, but it didn't matter, it was never good enough for him. Anna forgot that she used to set the standard. She forgot that his budget for her clothes wouldn't cover the back rack at an op shop. She tried so hard to please him, and to avoid the critical appraisal before they left. The drive to the event was always a tirade of abuse. He didn't know why he put up with her – she was so inadequate.

What amazed Anna was that George could tear her to shreds, then arrive at the event with all the dignity and superiority of a world authority on everything.

Anna longed for his approval, yet it never came. She, who had had so much flair and individuality, began to slide into lifelessness. It never occurred to her that in trying to meet George's unreachable standards, she had forsaken her own. In accepting the responsibility to make him proud of her, she never questioned who he was to set rules for her.

Cheshire Cats are really sad little alley cats. They aren't really alive at all. They are like old photos, staring out, afraid to move in case they blur their image. Like most of us, they are trying to survive in a critical world. Their strategy for survival is to appoint themselves judges of everything. They move in quickly to set the standards and suddenly you feel exposed. If you look intimidated, it's an open invitation to them to ridicule and abuse you. In learning how to handle such a vicious little pussy cat, you can free yourself from a lot of pain.

Cheshire Cats don't actually do very much at all. That would leave them exposed to the ridicule of others, and they won't risk that. They are very fragile because playing God without the talent or experience can be very stressful. They are modern Mona Lisas, with their little smile of inner knowingness, while being judgmental and intolerant. They are incredible frauds covering their failure: to act, to succeed and to know the joy of a trusting relationship and produce outstanding results. It's wasted knowledge. Everything is pretence.

The Cat will give you distorted information in a voice that rings with authority. Most of us are afraid of looking foolish, so we sit in silence trying to look casual. If you genuinely explore what they know it amounts to very little. They'll give you highlights and a reference but avoid discussion. They fear exposure and cover their fear with bravado, usually implying that you don't know enough to interest them. Don't counter-attack – you'd be threatening a fragile child, and when threatened, the cat withdraws, as if it is the end of a papal audience.

Like the rest of us, the Cheshire Cat has a need for recognition. If the Cheshire Cat is holding forth on a subject about which you know little, confess to confusion and ask for enlightenment. Never assume that the others present understand, because they are sitting there assuming you understand. Everyone hides in silence and embarrassment, giving the Cheshire Cat control. In our culture, we are afraid to admit that we don't know something – watch how the Cheshire Cat takes advantage of that fear.

It was a new company. They headhunted top performers from the profession, every one with a track record of innovative ability. The leader was young, but Grace had an impressive list of qualifications and she'd been associated with some of the biggest names in the industry.

At the first meeting, Grace listened for a while, then leaned forward and said, 'Let's be serious here. You can't be out-standing performers with such mediocre knowledge.'

They thought they were leading the field until she systematically tore their ideas to shreds. Grace wouldn't argue; she poked fun at their capability with cutting ridicule.

They felt exposed and they shrivelled into silence. It wasn't as if they had anything to argue against – Grace had contributed nothing. She would test their knowledge with obscure information no-one had heard of. They glanced at each other. None of them felt that they were up to her level of intellect. When she left the organisation, she left them in tatters. They never really knew what had happened to them, why they hadn't fulfilled their promise.

Grace moved on, leaving destruction and depressed people in her wake. Her CV was so impressive, no-one thought of checking what she actually produced.

Cheshire Cats create the same destruction in relationships. They expect their partners to be impressive. They usually pick spontaneous people, those who have the liberation they lack. They are attracted to those they believe are intelligent equals who they find stimulating, then proceed to pick them apart. The Cats make the rules, and if you let them, your life will be hell. Cats will find fault with the way you dress, what you say, how you say it.

How do Cheshire Cats get so much control? You allow it. Yet, the more you comply, the more anxious they feel. If you submit, they feel a moment of power, then dismiss you as being weak. Weakness in a partner could blemish the Cat's illusion of being powerful in all things. Part of that illusion is choosing a partner of note. If the partner submits to Cat control, the Cat's anxiety rises in direct proportion.

Albert collected degrees and titles the way some of us buy magazines. He belonged to everything. When he arrived to join our service club, it was like the parting of the waves. Everyone deferred to him. It was the end of life as we knew it. It wasn't that he said anything. In fact, thinking back on it, he never contributed at all. Albert always looked appalled at whatever he was hearing. Someone would suggest an idea and he would look directly at that person with pure amazement and disdain.

We colluded by our silence. Any suggestion made by any of us was accompanied by a quick glance at Albert to seek approval, yet it never came. All he had to do was make a few cynical remarks and we felt inadequate. There we were, prominent people in our own right acting like kids caught with our fingers in the cookie jar.

We were working on a fund-raising event one night. Albert was in the midst of annihilating a member with cutting sarcasm, when a voice behind him spoke up.

'So you don'ta like his idea? Wadda's your idea?' The voice was calm, curious and had a ring of certainty.

We turned in astonishment. Gina was an Italian migrant who had brought up a large family on her own. We had helped her kids get a higher education. In return, she insisted on making the coffee and cleaning up when we met. There she was, hands on her hips, standing right behind him, smiling away. 'Are you addressing me, madam?' the illustrious one asked in an icy tone.

'Sure you,' she said. It was clear she wasn't going to go away. 'You knock dat guy down, now wadda your idea?'

Albert gave Gina a withering glance, then turned his back on her. In a flash, she had grabbed his chair and spun him around as if she was giving him a fun ride. 'Come on, now,' she cajoled, 'Wadda you tink? Wadda you wanna do?' She didn't yield an inch.

'How dare you!' Albert gasped. 'I don't have to take this,' he said with as much poise as he could muster. He rose to his feet and made a dignified, if hurried retreat.

We could see him glance back as if he expected us, any of us, to stop him. Nobody moved. We turned to Gina in disbelief.

She smiled happily and said, 'Wat I tell my kids is, you donna play the game, you donna make the rules! You donna wanna let freeloaders in dis club now, do you. You do good tings! Now go get dat boy back and be nice. Teach him da game, but donna let him play durdy.'

The more confident you are in doing your own thing, the less Cheshire Cats will attack. Acknowledge their store of knowledge constantly – they have great difficulty attacking anyone who shows them genuine respect. If they try to discount you, ask them questions. Don't let them fob you off. Next time they'll do their homework, because they know you will ask for in-depth information and references.

You are not trying to trap them or humiliate them by asking a simple, curious question. You are not putting them on the spot. Leave them room for saving face by adding 'when you have time'. They have the choice of escaping or impressing you with valid information! They will more than likely do their homework.

If you are a Cheshire Cat's partner, trying to meet their standards is the worst thing you can do. That's walking right into their cage, and they will devour you. Fighting them, or trying to expose them, is bullying, and is beneath you.

Keep pursuing Cheshire Cats as the source of enlightenment, not to expose them, but to get them to share a seed of knowledge that they may have stored. Test them with gentle, genuine, unflustered, unflappable, tranquil curiosity. If they do choose to share what they know, their contribution will be impeccable. The real key to stopping Cats is to enjoy their storehouse of tidbits.

Ben and Donna were entertaining Ben's boss. Unfortunately, the boss was bringing his notorious wife. The wife was known to adore ripping other people's taste to shreds. Ben didn't know how he was going to protect his wife without attacking the woman known as Vampira.

He shared his anxiety with Donna. She looked at him gently, then questioned whether or not his real worry was that she couldn't handle it. She'd picked it.

He spluttered, 'Well nobody does!'

Donna assured him that she had survived an aunt who was similar and had learned a lot.

Nevertheless, Ben made his mind up that his job wasn't worth the aggravation. He'd let Vampira have it the minute she opened her mouth. He didn't have long to wait. Jessica sailed in, looked at their hall table and said, 'Isn't this ugly!'

Before he could draw breath, Donna had hooked her arm around Jessica and was guiding her into the next room as she said with a genuine laugh, 'Aren't you glad you don't own it!'

Over dinner Jessica made one last attempt to demolish her hostess. She poked at the dessert and announced, 'This tastes awful!'

Donna just smiled and said, 'Don't eat it!' but didn't offer a substitute. Vampira ate the dessert without further comment.

Never take a Cheshire Cat's criticism personally. See their negativity as the tip of the cesspool sloshing within them. Refuse to be affected by their insults. They are like little kids trying to impress. Help them by not taking them seriously, but don't stoop to ridicule or entrapment.

Christopher needed a partner to bask in his glory, so he married for the fifth time. His former partners had all had potential, but proved to be flawed under his scrutiny. It wasn't long before he and Kelly had to attend a big occasion together. As she was getting dressed, he circled around her. The pecking began, but he didn't get very far.

She kissed him on the forehead and said happily, 'Tell you what darling, you take responsibility for you, I will take responsibility for me. If you don't like my choices, don't look, or hoist a sign declaring "I am not with this woman".'

For the first time in his life Christopher felt secure. He actually had a good time. Kelly's freedom to do her own thing began to defuse the fear within him. She never let his fear contaminate her. Without being aware of it, he almost purred.

HELPING CHESHIRE CATS PLAY IN THE SUN
• Cheshire Cats are cold, detached and very destructive, projecting an image of superior intelligence. Don't you believe it!
• They are very judgmental and have a need for recognition. Be sure you give it if they've earned it.
• The more confident you are in your dealing with Cheshire Cats, the less they will attack.
• Question them if they criticise but don't put them on the spot. Give them room to resolve the situation.
• Treat Cheshire Cats with gentle, genuine, unflustered, unflappable, tranquil dignity and respect.
• The key to stopping a Cheshire Cat in its tracks is to enjoy and agree with their criticism. You're supposed to be

embarrassed, not happy! So be happy!

• Remember that they are little children trying to impress you, and they experience a great deal of stress. Hold your body rigid for three minutes and you'll know how they feel every day. They need to go to bed early – rigor mortis while breathing is exhausting!

• Use their valuable information. When you want research done, invite a Cat. Send them out to learn more. They won't dare to be less than outstanding.

• Remember to give them a standing ovation.

MARY HAD A LITTLE LAMB

(AND KILLED IT WITH KINDNESS)

Mary had a little lamb,
Its fleece was white as snow;
And everywhere that Mary went
The lamb was sure to go.

Be wary of Mary – she is Dracula's counterpart, operating in full daylight. She kills with kindness. She gains control by gently encouraging us not to trust our judgment, making us dependent on her. She thinks when you feel incompetent and incapable of learning, she will become important in your life. She will take over and rescue you when you don't need rescuing. She will advise you what to do whether you've asked for her help or not. She can subtly undermine your confidence until you are encased in doubt and she seems to be the only light at the end of the tunnel. If you discuss a problem with her, she is sure to solve it for you. She can sap your self-esteem, lull you into insensibility, leaving you in a deadly stupor of no confidence. You have to stop her before you become eroded. You are going to become aware of where kindness and body-snatching overlap. Your life is yours to control. With Mary you need to learn to set boundaries, thank her, and not bruise the relationship. If she insists on devouring you, say goodbye.

Isobel was the daughter of a very talented woman. She lived in her mother's shadow. It wasn't that her mother didn't encourage her – she did! Isobel remembered the day of her 18th birthday. Instead of a wrapped parcel, Gloria gave her daughter an envelope in which there was a credit card, allowing her to charge things to her parent's account at a very expensive department store.

'There you are, my darling,' said Gloria lovingly, 'your own credit card. This is the year you are going to start choosing your own wardrobe. I want you to start with a blouse. Hang the expense, but leave the tags on it until you are sure it's right. Developing good taste takes time, you know.'

Isobel felt a surge of independence as she approached the beautifully displayed blouses in the store. There was so much to choose from. Suddenly, she felt very unsure. Her mother was able to rush through a store skilfully grabbing this to go with that. The result was always stunning.

Isobel tried to take her time in choosing, but every time a salesperson approached her she felt afraid. What if she looked inept? She had a sense of panic that the assistant would see how unskilled she was. It was like a game of cat and mouse. The assistant would approach from one side of the display, Isobel would quickly move to the opposite side, but it drained her energy from the joy of choosing the blouse.

She summoned up her courage and said she was just look- ing. She had bought a moment's peace and she felt in control. Finally, she spotted it. A lovely soft cream blouse. It was simple and elegant. It called to her! She carried it home with great joy.

'I knew you could do it,' said her mother with enthusiasm. 'Try it on! No, don't take the tags off until we have a good look at it.'

Gloria circled her, sizing it up very carefully. Isobel waited anxiously for the verdict. 'It's really beautiful, but do you think it's the right colour for your skin?'

Isobel had a sinking feeling looking in the mirror. How could she have thought it was fine? But then she didn't have her mother's elegant taste.

'I'll take it back,' she said, feeling stupid.

'No, darling,' her mother said reassuringly. 'Let's take our time and see if it is salvageable.'

And that's how it went. Every day her mother insisted that she try it on for inspection.

Day two: 'It's hard to know how it will fit in with the rest of your wardrobe, darling, still it is your first choice.'

Day three: 'It's not a serviceable fabric is it? But we all make mistakes when we are starting out.'

Day four: 'Do you think it's appropriate for your age?'

Day five: 'Considering how little you are going to be able to wear it, do you think it's value for money?'

Day six: Isobel took it back.

The lovely Mary has a mission to help you, whether you want to be helped or not. She likes being helpful, believing in her superiority. Mary operates democracy her way.

In being helpful, Mary feeds her own sense of importance, brilliance, competence and unique ability. She believes that she is the ultimate authority on everything. You are in grave danger of not existing at all, if you don't recognise that she is trying to live your life for you. In this situation, you can experience guilt because you feel ungrateful towards someone who contributes so much to you.

Mary usually has no conscious, malicious intent. She just loves making decisions and one life doesn't seem to be enough. The more you allow her to decide for you, the less she respects you and the more she will discount your opinion. She is subtly competing with you on every front, expecting to win every time.

It never occurs to her that in imposing her way as being much better than yours, she really doesn't value us at all.

Keeping you as a helpless lamb creates the belief within her that she has a kind, generous, nature and is helping you to help yourself. This is not so: you don't even have to ask for her help, she just moves in. We learn by trying, but Mary won't let you try. Mary thinks she is being encouraging by always asking what you think, then gently and systematically disposing of your opinion. You can feel as if you're under local anaesthetic, hearing her from a distance.

Geoff had just taken over a new section of the company. It was the first time he had held a management position, but he'd read all the books. He got his team together and said that he'd welcome their contributions and that they could achieve miracles if they used each other's resources.

The team welcomed his openness because they had experienced a lot of blatant 'Do-it-my-way' managers in the past. Geoff was very helpful, approachable and friendly. They poured out their ideas to him. He always responded with, 'That's great', then gently told them why it wouldn't work. They were left feeling exposed. He smiled benignly.

There were times when Geoff countered them, even though he seemed to be saying the same thing in a different way. He would cut any idea down before it could breathe with a gentle summation of why it was not logical, realistic, professional or at the level of his expectation. Soon they learned to shut up.

It was 'Democracy My Way' to a slow waltz. He was very disappointed. It seemed no matter how much he encouraged them, they never opened their mouths. 'Hard to find commitment in people,' he told his wife.

You need to ask yourself some questions. Is Mary really interested and supportive of your ideas? Is there any evidence that she genuinely seeks your opinion and values it? Does she explore options with you, leaving you to make the decision? Or does she play a paternalistic judge and jury? Does she ever question her judgment or assumption that you are inexperienced or inferior and, therefore, in need of her experience, judgment and wisdom?

Does she consider whether what she wants would be of value to you or does she simply take over? How good is she at encouraging you to trust your own judgment? Does she encourage you, then systematically take your decision apart? How often is your influence sought?

You can end up feeling inadequate, while she feels vastly superior – and helpful!

Nick and Rachel were in love and decided to move in together, into Rachel's house. That first night Nick got home before Rachel and he opened the door to her, shouting, 'Surprise! Close your eyes'. He led her into the kitchen and happily said, 'Open up'.

She was horrified! He had completely rearranged all the contents of her kitchen cupboards. She stood with her mouth open as he told her joyously that he'd tackled her inefficiency.

She couldn't find the right pot for a week.

Rachel felt ungrateful; Nick was trying to be helpful. How lucky could she be?

A week later there was another surprise. This time, it was her extensive bookcase. All the carefully organised themes for her research had disappeared into alphabetical order. He purred with contentment.

Nick should never have attacked her cosmetics!

It might have been an excellent relationship if Rachel had stopped him at the kitchen. She let Nick encroach on her territory and he took it as permission to take complete control – of her! In her house!

Fortunately, Rachel had enough strength to rebel, and was on the way to learning the skills to stop him, setting up boundaries and getting on with building a good relationship.

You have to learn to stop Mary. If you don't keep control, honour your right to choose and maintain your right to learn, you may never feel a sense of competence. Welcome input from others, but the final decision should be yours. It may be scary at times, but life is about learning.

Thank Mary for her input, but be very clear about retaining control of choice. You don't have to argue. Smile and keep repeating, 'Thanks for the suggestions, I'll let you know what I decide'. If what you do doesn't have a satisfactory outcome, keep control of your learning too. Work out what's next. A friend doesn't say 'I told you so'. A manipulator does.

You may have to take Mary by the hand, sit her down and get her to listen because she is competing with everything you do. She is the body-snatcher who thinks your house, job, garden and children are up for grabs – but they're not!

It's sometimes difficult to have a conversation with Mary. As I've already pointed out, her expertise knows no bounds. She has an opinion on everything, she dissects everything you say, then follows with a better solution. If she could, she would eat for you!

What does Mary get out of so much control? She is nurturing herself at your expense! She truly believes she is smarter. The difficulty is that she gives advice with such generosity that you're afraid of hurting her feelings. If you don't define your boundaries clearly, she can be like a plague of locusts. Don't confuse love with being smothered; love does not smother. Love treasures your differences with respect.

An advertisement showed prominent women being phoned by the important men in their lives – fathers, husbands, lovers, brothers. Each man was suggesting that the woman couldn't take care of herself.
'Is my little girl taking care of herself?' they asked.
Each woman whispered softly, 'Thank you for caring about me'.

Control through concern is not caring. Real caring assumes people have the intelligence to work it out for themselves or find out what information they need.

When the message is 'You need me! Without me, you are nothing', you need to work out who is pulling the strings. If you allow it, you are losing confidence in direct proportion to the amount of control Mary has over you.

David felt very comfortable coming home and discussing work with his partner Peta. She loved it, feeling a part of his day and his decisions. He didn't notice it at first, but David started to feel uncomfortable discussing his day and he wasn't sure why. He felt himself withdrawing when she asked about work. He decided to pay attention to what she was doing that made him feel uptight.
It didn't take him long before he had it. He liked to talk about things while he weighed up the options. Every time he did, she would leap in with solutions. They were her solutions, but she was not offering them as possible alternatives. She was telling him what to do, her tone of voice suggesting that she knew better than he did.

Peta's language was immediately, 'You should...', 'You can't...', 'You have to...', 'Well, there is only one thing to do!...'

David felt hemmed in. He loved her interest, her involvement and he loved her. He didn't love her solving his problems.

David thought about it for a long time and finally he said, 'I like to talk about my problems with you and I like you listening. I appreciate the fact that you are trying to help me, but I love making my own decisions. I like it when you ask, "What about..." or "Would it be possible to...". I take that as exploring ideas, rather than you telling me how to do it. If it involves you, I promise that we will kick ideas around together until we both get what we want. Okay?'

As well as being partners, they've become best friends.

You can acknowledge Mary's contribution, but the final decision must rest with you. If it doesn't work out, you'll fix it. If you don't keep control and trust your own judgment, you can end up being underestimated or smothered. You'll feel as if you belong in the womb!

You don't need to wage a war to stop Mary's domination. Gentle humour is a clear message that is non-threatening. When you want input, ask her, thank her, then withdraw to consider your choices. Have patience. Mary loves making decisions and loves to jump in. Allow her to contribute to your decision making process, but not to take charge. Don't confuse love with smotherhood. Contribute? Yes! Take over? No! Stop them at the border – your border.

MAKE MARY A REFERENCE POINT, NOT THE CHAIRMAN OF THE BOARD

• Mary drains your confidence and orchestrates feelings of inadequacy by constantly undermining your decisions. She needs to be needed.

• Trust your own judgment and make your own decisions. How else can you learn?

• Thank Mary for her contribution, but inform her that the final decision is yours. You'll let her know how it turns out.

• Use gentle humour to relay your message. No need to reject or avoid someone who wants to belong.

• When you want input from Mary, ask for her advice, but the minute she makes a takeover move, tell her she'll have to wait for the next instalment.

LITTLE JACK HORNER

THE KNOW-IT-ALL, DO-IT-ALL LONERS

Little Jack Horner sat in a corner,
Eating his Christmas pie;
He put in his thumb,
And pulled out a plum,
And said, what a good boy am I!

Either Jack Horner sees everyone as competitors or he doesn't see us at all. Jack Horner has to prove he is the greatest. He behaves like an adolescent, flexing his muscles. This encourages him to be brave enough to stand up and be counted. Long ago, Jack Horner decided to survive and own his life, but it can be a lonely journey. Winning helps him feel more secure and more powerful temporarily. His fear of being beaten or not being recognised for achievement and individuality drives him to keep moving at full speed. It's hell when he loses, but that doesn't stop him having another go. He craves recognition even more than winning, while being afraid that satisfaction will drop him into stagnation. He sees people as being either a threat or inadequate: he makes enemies of us all. You probably don't give him the recognition he craves because he doesn't treat you as significant. In fact, you can be tempted to thwart him if you can get away with it, but it isn't a way to control him. You need him to stop his abuse without losing his talents. You are going to help him win because he has much to contribute in the way of enthusiasm and talents. You are going to give him deserved recognition because from his courage and achievements, you can start developing your own talents, gain his trust and, in the process, discover your potential. You can form a mutual support team once Jack recognises your value.

Brett was a high achiever, a master at everything he tried. He was only 30-something, but you could believe he'd lived 50 lifetimes, he was so talented.

He soon found the girl he wanted to marry. Susan was tall, elegant, articulate and excellent with people. She only had to walk into a room and every head turned in her direction. The only drawback was that she was not from a notable family. Still, she had gained prominence in her own right, and she was malleable. Yes, Susan was the girl for him.

He picked her up for dinner in the Rolls Royce. The Ferrari wasn't appropriate for this occasion. Quiet elegance was the right mood for a night like this. He'd picked the finest restaurant and, as they swept up the stairs, the staff welcomed him by name. The head waiter assured him that the wine he had ordered was chilled exactly to the temperature he'd requested.

They were ushered to their table, the one Brett had ordered, semi-sheltered, but sufficiently prominent to be noticed. The aperitif was poured and he went through the proper ritual of noting the colour, temperature, bouquet. He didn't glance her way, but he was sure that Susan was impressed with his knowledge in conversation with the wine waiter. He told her he had designed their meal from start to finish. With every course, he went through the wine ritual and gave her a casual lecture on the food, the sauces, the mysterious blend of flavours, and how he was the only non-professional to be invited to study in some of the world's greatest wine districts.

During the meal, he tested her on political, scientific and

international issues of importance. She did not falter. She was fully informed and, to his surprise, added some information of which he was not aware. She was open, charming and intelligent, as well as being the most beautiful woman in the room.

His timing was impeccable. He produced the ring shortly after coffee. He'd designed it. It was big enough to impress, but not over the top, just a lovely hint of things to come. He told her that she was everything he wanted in a wife, and with her at his side, the world was theirs.

His eyes met hers and, to his horror, she laughed as she shoved the ring back at him. To his embarrassment, other diners looked around and a few heard her say, 'Don't be ridiculous, you don't even involve me in the choice of food I am going to eat'. She swept out of the restaurant before he could catch his breath.

Brett quickly pocketed the ring and forced himself into serious calm, which is difficult for a Jack Horner. 'Lots more fish in the sea,' he purred as he quickly recovered his composure.

The ring did not go to waste. He found a more suitable candidate and was engaged some three weeks later. He loved making it happen.

Jack Horner is a self-driven, self-motivated, courageous loner. He is the innovator, the pathfinder, the one who takes the risks, but he is also a predator who tries to kill off any competitor. Jack rarely knows the rest of us exist unless he needs us; then he notices us. But we're not dumb – we know we are being used, and that's how Jack creates enemies.

Arrogance and superiority mask his fear of failure. He is always trying to prove his superiority and individuality. Jack

Horner is terrified of being confused with anybody else; he is a rampant individual. He is trying to discover who he is and who he could be. You see him as self-assured and confident because he has an insatiable drive to prove that he is the best. Many Jack Horners have been abused in the past, perhaps by parents who said they weren't smart enough to do anything; or they may have been ridiculed when they didn't achieve everything they said they would.

Instead of accepting defeat, Jack chooses to be an unstoppable survivor! We choose to abuse him by calling him a 'show-off' and 'know-it-all' and we sabotage him every chance we get. Envy and competition hurt Jack, but also bring out his courage, turning fear into action. He knows through experience that most things he fears don't happen, so he gets even. This generates resistance in us, and the war goes on.

How does he react to your rejection? 'I'll show you!' he screams from his soul. As he soars over your head, he can't resist plopping his droppings on you.

But he needs you, and you need him. He can help you come out of the dark shadows of your own fear, provided you are smart enough to learn from him. First, give him the recognition he deserves, then stop his abusive behaviour by withholding cooperation until he values it. You must tell him what the options are, or he has no opportunity to learn. It is hard for you to give him recognition, because he is unlikeable. You may also suffer from ingrown envy, especially if you are sitting on your own potential. It would be smarter to make a friend of Jack Horner, build trust and discover that you can acknowledge his achievements after all.

Jack will always discount your perceptions, so you will have lots of practice in stopping him when he abuses you. Don't accept any put-downs. Withdraw cooperation if he abuses you in any way. Nobody has the right to question your opinion. Stop his ridicule, barbed humour and personal attacks in a comfortable way. 'Put me down and you lose a friend, Jack' works well. Never argue with a Jack Horner; tangling with his aggression will only get you bruised. He has to win and that need may dominate his judgment and emotional control.

You are offering what Jack needs most – support! That support only comes if Jack treats you with respect. Remember how your parents taught you to ask nicely and say 'please' and 'thank you'? If he wants a relationship with you, he has to play by those rules. Let him know that if he breaks them, he doesn't get your cooperation.

Yet respect is far more than polite conversation. It means your needs are considered as significant, too. Justice for all is the foundation of a relationship. Jack Horner is so involved with himself that you will need to be prepared to spell out the rules calmly and frequently. Keep offering help; it's worth it.

Smile comfortably, wave your hand and walk away as soon as a personal attack begins. If he makes a demand, walk yourself around the block. It's not a silence attack. Counter with a simple, direct 'Ask me! Don't tell me!' A demand is taking away your right of choice; a request leaves you room to meet your needs as well as Jack's. Repeat your manifesto – no respect, no cooperation – and mean it. The more comfortable you are at waving goodbye if you are deluged by sarcasm, ridicule or demands, the more he will learn. He has to play nice!

Many people are quick to put competitive people down when they fail. It's called 'Tall Poppy Lopping'. Jack takes poppy lopping as a challenge. Jack Horner spills over with the joy of achievement. You may call it boasting, but enjoy his celebration and learn from it. If you genuinely acknowledge Jack Horner's positive impact, you will win his trust. Poor Jack needs to come in from the cold to discover your talents. You need to tell Jack what you have to offer, and you need to be valued, included and given recognition for your part. If he begins to value you and include you in his adventures, you can discover Jack Horner's world of confidence.

Acknowledge his courage, that he will pick himself up, dust himself off and start all over again. Going beyond failure is courage. You need to be specific in your feedback, because although he wants recognition most of all, he finds it difficult to accept. He also finds it difficult to relax and enjoy his achievements. Jack Horner thinks that if he ever relaxes and enjoys his achievements, he may stop achieving. He's like a little animal on a treadmill – massive output, no joy! You can help Jack to learn to love his journey. When he is trying so hard to prove how great he is, he can be incredibly insensitive towards the needs of others. Learn how to stop him. You are the best thing to help him come in from isolation and start living.

Lynn, a Super Jack Horner, clawed her way to the top of her field, over mountains of bodies. Her partner Matthew managed his own successful business and backed her all the way. He was proud of her. Foolishly, Lynn took him for granted. The more she felt under pressure, the more she demanded of him. Whatever he did was never enough. She poured all her inner demons over his head like molten lava. Matthew warned her to back off, but she didn't listen.

One night Lynn found him sitting in a chair, reading. The meal wasn't ready. The rule was whoever got home first, cooked. (She was never home first.) She roared while he looked and listened. When there was a lull, Matthew said calmly, 'I'm leaving you'.

Lynn's response was, 'Don't be ridiculous!'

'Would you like to know why?' he asked calmly.

'I refuse to talk to you,' Lynn said and stomped into the kitchen. She waited there, but he didn't come. She went back to him, tantrum ready.

'Would you like to know why?' Matthew repeated. She realised he was serious. He told her that the love, respect, support and recognition he provided she mistook as her right and his weakness. She didn't understand the power of kindness. She never reciprocated and instead used him as a dumping ground.

Lynn screamed, 'Go! I don't need you. I don't need anybody!' She assumed he would give in. He always had in the past when he attempted to balance the power between them, but this time he didn't. He looked at her in a detached way, as if he was waiting for a bus, and said, 'If you are interested in sharing, give me a call'.

She took bets on how quickly he'd return, but she lost them all. She told everyone she didn't give a damn, but she did. He gave her nothing to fight with. There were no arguments, no recriminations, no discussions about the past. He had simply said that if there was to be a future, it was to be built on sharing and respect. He left the choice to her.

In his absence, she discovered that fury and ambition didn't keep her warm at night. She became aware that she took his kindness as her due, never considering his needs. She took a big step. She invited him to dinner. Matthew came but was clear about what he wanted – no temper tantrums, no bullying, no demands, no put-downs and no criticism, just two-way interest, contribution and cooperation. If she reverted to the demanding tirades he would withdraw cooperation.

She didn't stop achieving, nor did he. Years later she was

still saying, 'Thank God you gave me a chance'.

Love and cooperation are not weaknesses, they are gifts. Jack Horner would like to come in from the cold of isolation. He is out there on the cliff face, knowing that the world would cheer if he fell. It isn't a good feeling.

In setting limits, you help him discover that his drive is a creative force, but as long as he stomps on other's needs, he won't get the support and recognition he needs. He can have it all: outstanding achievement, recognition and support, and he will probably live longer once he doesn't have to crush you along the way. You aren't the enemy, and you aren't him. Jack will achieve greater results when he has your backing, but he must consider your needs and your potential in order to get cooperation. You are not an 'also ran' – and you must be specific about what you can contribute to his achievements.

You may fear loss of financial support if you set limits on Jack by leaving. What price are you willing to pay for this amount of stress in your life? If you don't stop him abusing you, he has no reason to change. If he left you, or you left a job, you'd probably take a deep breath of fresh air and learn to manage on your own.

In offering cooperation on your terms, you are stopping his abuse but not attacking him. You are one big healthy 'STOP' sign, and that is more productive than a war. Toughness is choosing not to fight, drawing a line on your availability while still offering a positive relationship.

Jack Horner's need to control and win is so massive that sometimes he operates close to the edge of emotional control. If you fear physical attack, get out, and get help. Your protection is then your first and only consideration. If he does attack you physically, go to the legitimate authorities and press charges.

Follow through and deliver the consequences. Jack needs professional help and you can't help him. He can't help himself and needs external support if he's going to turn his life around. For his sake and yours, deliver the consequences. If you don't act, Jack will take it as an empty threat and assume that he's won again. Every time you let him get away with abusive behaviour, both of you lose: you in confidence and he in emotional control. Never counter-attack.

With Jack, winning is everything, and he can lose perspective. In these conditions, he has no respect for you. You are the one to teach him that he'll get what he wants faster if he recognises how valuable you are and that you deserve his respect. You will get stronger the more you value yourself. Taking a risk to trust anybody is the most fearful thing for a fierce competitor to do. Jack Horner is so fragile inside; he needs a few chances.

You can learn a lot from a Jack. He can teach you to use failure as simply part of the learning process. Failure gives him the tools for new directions. Your gift to him will be to teach him that he can achieve even more with your support. He won't stagnate in peace and harmony unless he chooses to do so, and achievement doesn't have to be a life or death struggle. If he put that same persistence into an emotionally balanced relationship, it wouldn't erode his individuality. Two strong, independent people, choosing to retain their individuality *and* work together, can create miracles.

Comparison and competition keep Jack Horner afraid. You can help him appreciate who he is. If you do, he'll no longer have to prove he is the greatest; he can get on with being great, appreciating his journey and your talents.

Nina and Anthony were two powerful journalists working for competing papers. What one did, the other topped. They were extremely clever at discounting each other. They came dangerously close to libel.

Nina's paper offered Anthony a sum he could not ignore to join them. He thought it would be an ideal position from which to eradicate Nina.

Nina screamed and kicked, threatening to quit. The managers assured her that competition was more profitable and more easily controlled within.

What management bought was chaos. The two were so busy upstaging each other that their work came off second best and circulation dropped. Management hauled them onto the carpet and screamed abuse, failing to understand that competition is a dangerous thing to unleash, especially on home turf.

The following day, Nina walked up to the desk of her opposition. Everyone held their breath. 'I understand that you are working on that political scandal,' she said. Anthony stiffened, ready for a fight.

'I came across this information in my files,' she said. 'It's old, but I think it could provide you with some useful background.' She walked out calmly.

Anthony won a prestigious award for his story. At his acceptance he acknowledged Nina's contribution. They both rose to prominence and were sought after around the world. They still draw on each other's support no matter where they are.

TEACH JACK HORNER TO FLY RIGHT WITH YOU
- Jack Horner thrives on competition and recognition.
- Become his friend, build trust and acknowledge his talents rather than sabotaging him.
- Offer support on the condition that he treats you with respect, because you deserve it.

• Jack is poor at listening. Be prepared to spell out rules frequently: no respect, no cooperation.
• Walk away, if necessary, if Jack is pressuring you.
• Stand by your convictions. Jack needs to understand the meaning of a 'STOP' sign.

SLEEPING BEAUTY

(ALL THAT GLITTERS COULD BE

THE WRAPPING)

And now the king and the queen,
having kissed their dear child
without waking her
went out of the palace.
…There grew up all around about the park
such a vast number of trees, great and small,
that neither man nor beast could pass through.

OLD FRENCH TALE, ANDREW LANG COLLECTION

Sleeping Beauty can live a whole life without discovering who she is. Her identity is based upon being linked with very important people. She will chase a relationship where there is someone of money, fame or status, in order to bask in the reflection. She knows everybody who is anybody and is a classic networker. She will drop you if you run into hard times because she doesn't want to be associated with failure – it terrifies her. She is up-to-date with fashion, cars, holidays, foods, restaurants and who is with whom, but it's impossible to get behind the wrapping, to have an in-depth conversation with her. She will treat you as if you are the most important person in the world, then drop you if you provide a link to someone else she believes is more important. It can leave you wondering 'What's wrong with me?' Nothing – you have just experienced a relationship in which someone has used you as the rung of a ladder. If Sleeping Beauty needs you again she will be back, as if the relationship is still intact.

Should you put energy into this relationship? Well, it is possible to see Sleeping Beauty as a little kid, looking for permanent safety. She believes security comes in the shadow of importance. If someone she is clinging to sees through her façade, she can be bounced out of the inner circle. When she is rejected, you can provide the substance she needs in her journey to the discovery that safety lies within. Meet the fragile resident behind the hedge.

> Erin picked her friend, Amelia, up at the airport in a very expensive car. They hadn't seen each other since school and on the way home, Erin told her friend they would pick her kids up at school.
>
> Erin parked on a leafy street where there was no evidence of a school. 'How clever to park away from the school area,' said Amelia. 'Safety reasons?' she asked.
>
> 'Heavens, no,' was the reply. 'The kids wouldn't be caught dead in this old heap, they'd be embarrassed, it's a year old. I have to park out of sight, until we get something better.'

Sleeping Beauty is dressed at her best every day of the week. Everything she does is done to create an image. Her whole life is devoted to impressing the neighbours. She follows every trend, hoping to be nearly first, yet she never goes first. She puts enormous energy into a relationship with somebody who is somebody, following them devotedly. Meanwhile, who is she? She doesn't know, because every choice she makes is influenced by what others are doing or saying. She is there at the starting line, waiting for the gun to go off, but is afraid to go first.

She does not invest in herself. She is temporarily non-existent, sleeping in the shadows of successful people. It's tough on the illustrious people and the rest of us, because a Sleeping Beauty is so socially skilled it's hard to tell if she is true or false. They are skilful 'hangers-on'.

She will be with you only while you attain notable success. Should you fall from grace, she will never remember your name. This can hurt a lot if you take her rejection personally. Don't. She is a tender little kid trying to balance in big people's shoes. She believes that shadow dancing will keep her safe. It does, but at a price, because she is still fast asleep – an unborn self.

Sleeping Beauties can spot other Sleeping Beauties at a glance. They can be unscrupulous in attacking potential competition.

At a high-powered convention, a small group of notables and semi-notables were being introduced to each other. One man, in the middle of shaking hands, suddenly extended the arm of the man to whom he was being introduced. Glancing pointedly at the man's wristwatch he said, 'Good copy! Hong Kong?' They both smiled, but the battle lines were drawn.

It's very precarious walking on the edge of the success cliff. It can be threatening financially, too. Only the truly confident have the courage to admit to second-hand clothes or a copy watch. Only the truly confident pick external things because they suit them; trends are rarely a consideration. Sleeping Beauty is trapped in the cancerous cage of reflection, comparison and competition.

She plays at intimacy, and is very good at it, but the last thing she wants is to get close to anyone, because intimacy might allow someone to cut through the hedge that has grown up around her and discover that she is superficial, empty, frightened and fragile.

Jonathan and Natasha had been married for six years and had two lovely small children. Jonathan could never believe his luck. Natasha was so beautiful, so gracious. She deserved the best and he tried to provide it.

The long hours it took him to make the money she spent infuriated Natasha. She wanted him home at 6 pm and available for social engagements. She left him in no doubt that he was a very lucky man to have her and she constantly compared him unfavourably with the successes of others.

Jonathan couldn't understand why, when he loved her so much, he felt such a deep ache inside his chest as he drove home each night. He hadn't realised that anyone's best is never good enough for the Beauty. There is always someone on the horizon with more glitter.

One day Jonathan moved mountains to get home early, but when he arrived, Natasha wasn't there. He went to the phone to see if she'd left a message. She hadn't, but someone else had. The voice belonged to a mutual friend, a wealthy high-achiever. The intimacy of the voice, and the message, shocked him. He sat there, stunned, for a very long time. He was still sitting there when she arrived. He didn't respond to her, he just played the tape. She didn't deny she was having a relationship with someone else, didn't excuse it and didn't avoid it. She graciously told him that she didn't intend living with a low-achiever who couldn't even get home on time. She was gone by the weekend.

It took him a while to realise it, but the best thing was that Natasha had left the kids with him.

If Sleeping Beauty leaves you, her rejection can hurt you deeply, but it's not really you she's rejecting. A relationship with the Beauty has to be financially and socially secure, with the prospect of a more glittering future. Unfortunately there is always more glitter on the horizon.

You have to stop Sleeping Beauty's daily inspection tour. It can sap the confidence out of your body like a magnet. She'll check you from head to toe, hovering near to hear what you say and how you say it. This can put you in an unwinnable position if you are interested in being who you are rather than a copycat. Sleeping Beauty can be brutally critical of you and others. Her brilliant wit, a sign of creative potential, is used as a weapon to expose the soft spots of others. Walk away from it. Don't let it seep in.

If you run into problems, she panics, trying to dissociate herself from your failure, but you can learn a lot from Sleeping Beauty's abusive behaviour. The fear is hers – don't pick it up. The more Beauty rattles you, the more you must value your choices, your right to live your life according to your judgment, your right to continually experience the unknown. When you do this, you'll not only gain strength but you'll also see how fragile she is. The moment you take control of who you are and who you want to be is the moment she begins to value you. Sleeping Beauty stands in awe of people who are getting on with their lives, comfortably independent of social comparison and status. When you don't let her barbs wither you and you laugh at her humour without believing it, she begins to feel more secure with you. Sleeping Beauty cannot imagine the freedom of getting up in the morning and wondering 'What do I want to do today?' without worrying about the opinion of others.

Security is not something you can buy. It is born inside you the moment you see your life as yours, to learn, to enjoy and to walk the path you choose. Changing your mind at any time is your business.

One partner who helped her Sleeping Beauty grow up

suggested he carry a sign saying, 'I don't know who she is!' Learn to openly, directly and calmly stop critical comments from the Beauty. Easily and comfortably declare your intention to choose for yourself. Not everybody has to like oranges.

Let her arrogance blow away like the illusion that it is. Your freedom terrifies her, but deep inside she knows that if she is to be safe that is the route she must take. Your clarity in being who you are can give her a vision of what is possible in life if she has the courage to take that step. If you learn to stand by your choices calmly and comfortably, without anger and without being defensive, being near a Sleeping Beauty can help you develop your confidence a lot. It also helps her see maturity in action.

She must know that you are free to make your choices. The more you respect your right to choose who you are, independent of how others want you to be, the more you are upholding a basic human right. Have compassion and smile at her. Thank her for her input, while telling her what you are choosing to do, – then do it. If you find yourself reacting, go and look at yourself in a mirror and recover your poise. Great relationships meet both people's needs, and it's up to you to state yours.

Every time they were going out, Hayden became deeply agitated. He picked Bianca to pieces from top to toe, yet once they arrived, his agitation melted. He would become the delightful person she had married: popular and charming, with a brilliant sense of humour.

No matter where Hayden was, his eyes never left her. If Bianca didn't perform according to his standards, he would swoop down and vacuum her up. Hissing in her ear, while graciously smiling and nodding to others, Hayden would batter her with recriminations. How stupid, how inept she was!

'Mingle, mingle,' was his command as he pointed out the most important people in the room.

On the next big occasion Hayden was, as usual, outside in their car, hand on the horn, urging her to hurry. After ten minutes of horn-blasting, he strode back into the house, almost ripping the door off the hinges, screaming, 'What in hell do you think you're doing?'

She knew exactly what she was doing. A shower had levelled her beautifully styled hair and had taken her impeccable make-up with it. She was sitting up comfortably in bed with a book.

He went ballistic. She didn't appear to hear him. She went on reading, totally relaxed. When he had run out of steam, he heard just two words.

'Never again.' She meant it and he knew she meant it.

The rules for the future were laid out: no criticism, no verbal abuse, no demands. Only requests were acceptable. The view of each person would be taken into consideration. Her social occasions would be for making friends. They would not be for the purpose of impressing the neighbours. He could go off and do his own thing.

'I need you to front for me. If you aren't going to do that, we might as well separate,' he threatened.

'Okay,' she said and turned the page.

It suddenly hit him that the reason he had chosen her was because of her unconscious grace and acceptance of herself. He began to value her substance; he couldn't explain it, but he didn't feel as tense.

When Sleeping Beauty has a need to bask in the reflection of others' achievements, she may not be listening to her own needs. Unless she learns to give approval to herself, she will never be safe. Once she does approve of herself, she can help others learn to walk the road to individual growth.

Her loving acceptance and appreciation of herself, her calmness in creating her own solutions without hurting others, is the ultimate powerful impression. She doesn't have to apply it; it comes from within in the form of tranquillity.

Trusting yourself, and doing what it takes to get to where you want to be is maturity. It takes initiative, focus, discipline and enthusiasm. Seeking recognition as a result of association, without doing any of the hard work to get there, is precarious. It is like breathing without really living. Living is all about taking time to enjoy your choices. You are genuinely interested in others. You have the confidence to enjoy their difference, seek their opinion and coexist on mutual respect. When your laughter is a joyous expression from within, you own your life.

You can help Sleeping Beauty choose to give up intolerance and a desire to make you wear a wrapping that's the wrong fit. If you live by Beauty's demands, you are choosing a life of anxiety. The more anxious you become, the more insecure she feels with you. The more acceptance you give yourself, the more you live with respect. Acceptance of others is wonderful, but not your first priority.

If you take care of yourself, Sleeping Beauty might risk the unwrapping process – waking up and learning to deal with an unpredictable world. She must make the choice to cut through the hedge that has isolated her. If you have the compassion to still offer support, a very special relationship is possible. We all need a chance to make changes and to learn to try another road.

Elizabeth was an exceptionally beautiful person, inside and out. People would glance at her when she walked down the street. She was warm, friendly, open and natural, and everyone felt comfortable in her presence.

She fell in love with an upwardly mobile young executive and married him. The wedding was sensational. It wasn't long before Alexander started to recreate her. It was as if his attraction to her in the first place was a mistake. Her hair, make-up, walk, talk – everything was given a new mould.

Elizabeth's family watched in sadness as she tried to please him. The joy went out of her face: the smile was there, but her eyes were anxious, constantly checking to see if he approved. She never got approval. Alexander could be talking to a group of people across the room and still wither her with a reproving glance. Elizabeth lost all her spontaneity. Oh, she glittered, but it was superficial.

He rose! She froze! He was bitterly disappointed when she announced that she was expecting their first child. He asked for a divorce two weeks later. She was devastated.

Alexander was quick to choose his next partner. Elizabeth's family watched him gift-wrap her as well.

After a long period of grieving, Elizabeth re-emerged and became a very successful person in her own right. She walked tall again. Some years later, Alexander's company crashed and his current Sleeping Beauty took off, following more houses, more cars, a beach house and a yacht.

When Elizabeth invited Alexander to her home, everyone thought she was mad. He didn't emerge for some time, but when he did, he'd softened. She gathered old friends that he'd long forgotten. They acted as if he'd never been away. They got him involved in events, using his entrepreneurial skills. He rose again to prominence, but in quite a different way. He didn't forget his old friends. Everyone considered him a fortunate person.

LETTING LIGHT PENETRATE THE HEDGE

• Sleeping Beauty builds her identity through illusion and association, hoping that security will flow from the shadow of successful people. It doesn't!

• Basking in the reflection of other people's achievements means the Beauty must deny her potential. She believes she has to be a copycat to be a success.

• Learn to accept and appreciate yourself, despite being rejected by Sleeping Beauty. Anyone who rejects the opportunity of knowing you must have poor taste.

• By being a supportive friend, you can help Sleeping Beauty discover the glitter that has always been inside her.

THE LION AND THE UNICORN

(THERE IS NO POINT IN STEPPING INTO THE

MIDDLE OF A WAR!)

The lion and the unicorn
Were fighting for the crown;
The lion beat the unicorn
All around the town.
Some gave them white bread
And some gave them brown;
Some gave them plum cake,
And sent them out of town.

There is no way you are going to give these bullies bread or cake until they deserve it. No environment can afford them – not our homes, our community or our world. You are watching a war being waged without the privilege of switching channels. You must not allow them airplay. You are going to learn how to feel comfortable in the middle of the fray because you will know how to stop them. They are going to solve their differences and impress you. You don't want to diminish either one of them and you are not going to take sides. Your skill will be to show them how to constructively work together. They have to fix it and fast, whether they are two children at each other's throats or opposing forces at the office. You will not rescue or intervene, but you will deliver clearly defined consequences if they don't settle the conflict.

Molly was the mother of five children, so she wasn't intimidated when she walked into the meeting room and found two teams lined up with obvious tension between them. She was the newest member of the team. She smiled at them, but the men did not respond.

The meeting began and the gloves came off. They went for each other's throats. Each side had its champion head kicker and they sat opposite each other. No matter which side contributed, the other sneered and carved up the contribution. The chairperson tried to keep some semblance of control, but he lost dismally. Most people wished they were somewhere else.

Molly intervened and asked, 'Are you expecting contributions from everyone?'

'Be my guest,' said one champion with cynical graciousness. Everyone laughed, some feeling very uncomfortable that the lamb was heading for the slaughter.

When Molly made a suggestion they tried to shout her down. Instead she held up her hand like a traffic cop. She didn't seem to recognise the danger. 'You promised to listen,' she smiled, calmly confronting one bully.

'I did listen. Your idea won't work.'

'Fine. Tell me how you would make it work,' she said comfortably.

He couldn't.

Molly continued as if there had been no interruption.

'What I hear are two possibilities to solve the problem and I want to explore the potential of both of them,' she said. Apparently nobody had told her she wasn't chairing the meeting. When an idea was shot out of the water, Molly would turn to the shooter and ask them 'You have described a problem within that idea. How would you fix it?'

If that person couldn't, she threw it open to the entire group. When someone said, 'We tried that and it didn't work', Molly asked, 'What stopped you?' It didn't matter whether they said 'time', 'resources', or 'money', Molly would respond with, 'So, how do we get those resources if we want to do this?' She didn't seem to comprehend that there were limitations.

People who normally expected to count body blows, day-dream or do the crossword puzzle in these meetings started to contribute. By the end of the meeting, no-one thought that Molly had no authority. Both strategies had been fully developed, and everyone knew who was going to do what and by when. There had been participation and commitment, and it had taken only half an hour.

The two champions were stunned. Their ideas had been snatched, signed, sealed and delivered. They even got credit for originating the ideas. They couldn't understand why she wasn't threatened.

If they'd asked her, she could have told them that you have to keep your cool and focus when you are arbitrating between five kids all demanding centre stage. At the same time you have to teach them to solve the problem so everybody gets more than they hoped for.

Lions and Unicorns are really very brave. They are your modern equivalent of the gladiators in the Colosseum, choosing to die trying. They put themselves on the line every time someone suggests something. They are not interested in better ideas because they are trying to prove that they are better, more intelligent and more experienced than everyone else. Imagine trying to live up to that expectation in one lifetime. You can't afford them as they are, though. They destroy other people's ideas. They listen, but only to tell you how wrong you are. Do they help each other? No. Do they help their family, community, company, country? No. Do they share information? Absolutely not – they sit on it.

The Lion and Unicorn aren't interested in earning their pay – they use work as a competitive forum. They act like nine-year-olds dressed as grown-ups. They dismiss non-competitors as stupid and they love saying, 'I don't suffer fools gladly', which includes all of us. It's easy to sit back and let them fail, but it's a terrible waste in all directions.

Lions and Unicorns are afraid of being afraid. As soon as they feel fear, they keep up a blistering pace so it won't conquer them. You can tap into that energy and use it rather than waste it thinking up hundreds of ways to block their achievements.

Lions and Unicorns have little success in relationships because they are afraid of closeness. A partner might discover where they are vulnerable. Lions and Unicorns tend to die early from burnout. Partners have at least twelve years to spend the insurance and probably feel they deserve it. But no-one deserves to live through such constant trauma. In helping Lions and Unicorns, you help yourself.

How do you stop Lions and Unicorns? Your first step is to recognise how valuable you are to them. You know that they are both high achievers and that they can't make it without support even if they think they can. You are going to offer support but on your terms. You will help them succeed by offering cooperation only if they ask for it and only if they treat you with respect. Rehearse! Become so comfortable in your head with how you are going to tame them that what you say is direct, easy and natural. Instead of being intimidated, you have to say your cooperation is available only if they say 'please' and 'thank you'.

A tourist in Spain was enraged. His luggage had disappeared

and he roared at the airline staff surrounding him. They just stared. The more they stared, the more he roared in five languages. When he'd run out of steam, one of the staff members smiled gently at him and said 'You can have our help but only if you say "please"'.

You may not want to help a Lion or Unicorn but you have what they need most – your cooperation. Instead of being intimidated, you can help them develop social intelligence without blocking their creativity.

Expect to find a conversation with them very frustrating. Even when you are agreeing with them, they have to have the last word. Sometimes their tone of voice will be patronising; at other times expect a blatant, direct attack. When you expect bullying, it should lose its impact and you can focus instead on offering your support. Watch their faces the first time you ask if you can help. Expect them to say 'no' and to dress it up in the form of ridicule or some other type of verbal attack. Remember, you don't have to be intimidated or impressed, you're looking at a little kid, trying to be brave, going it alone.

What do you gain by helping Lions and Unicorns? You stop them being confidence killers and dangerous wasters of others' talent, time and resources. You will need to learn not to be intimidated by their abusive behaviour. The more comfortable you are in the presence of abuse, the safer you are. The purpose of intimidation is to frighten you. If you are comfortable and treat them with respect at all times, they may learn to trust you, but it doesn't matter if they do or don't.

John was one of the most influential men of his day. Every morning, he would buy a newspaper from a man noted for his obnoxious behaviour.

John would greet the newsagent, wish him good morning, request the paper he wanted, pay for it (he never had the right change), then wish the man a pleasant day. The purchase was made in a hail of expletives, which John never seemed to notice.

This infuriated his staff, but he would not let them buy him his paper for him, so they offered to threaten the newsagent.

This amused their boss, who said that the obnoxious man unwittingly trained him. John had seen a lot of abusive conflict and felt it hindered achievement. He'd discovered that he got further by treating people with respect, while focusing on the problem until a satisfactory conclusion for everyone had been reached.

For John, buying the paper in the morning was like going to the gym. After the paper routine he comfortably negotiated with the most powerful intimidators the world could deliver and they couldn't scare him a bit. John suggested that his staff focus on the newsagent. He told them to notice that although the expletives continued there wasn't much fire in them. It was all a facade to save face. His staff started to buy their own papers from the newsagent – it was too good an opportunity to miss.

The purpose of rage is to keep others under control. The key to handling bullies is not to react but to choose to act with respect and an offer to help them, making it difficult for them to continue the attack. You are in control. When the wind spills from their sails, be ready to help. Acknowledge their achievements – there will be many and they will begin to trust another human being who is not intimidated nor manipulative. They will begin to focus on producing outcomes, rather than proving how incredible they are. It is focusing their energy constructively.

Making fun behind their backs reinforces your powerlessness – they are in control.

You are in control of your own method of response. The greatest impact you can have is to treat others with genuine respect, while acknowledging and using their talents. If you respond to them by arguing or putting them down, then you have resorted to their tactics.

If you discover a Lion or Unicorn working for you, you need to lay down your expectations about how they will deal with other people. Draw a line in the sand at the first sign of bullying or ridicule. Take them aside and tell them that you expect everyone to be treated with courtesy: workmates, clients or people passing through. If not, you must assume that they have not yet developed the social intelligence skills to interact with dignity. Only when they achieve that level of intelligence will you offer to help them achieve. If they aren't willing to develop those skills, they are in the wrong organisation.

You can set Lions and Unicorns an inspirational goal that would seem impossible to achieve. Remember, proving how brilliant they are is what drives them to compete. If they choose not to cooperate with each other, tell them that you'll look for other resources. Take away their chance to excel and you will have their undivided attention.

A family that competes or compares is likely to produce Lions and Unicorns. It's as unacceptable as setting fire to the house. Playing, not fighting, is how children learn to be socially intelligent in interacting with others. They must learn to resolve the conflict between themselves so that everyone gets a fair share. When most parents say 'calm down' or discount the fights as 'normal' behaviour, they are not setting limits on unacceptable behaviour. Set the limits and tell them what they stand to lose if they don't cooperate. This is teaching children to be accountable for their behaviour.

Bridget's two sons never stopped fighting. She tried to be the peacemaker but she gave in when either one of them screamed 'Not fair!' She didn't want to be unfair, so she tried to sort out the facts instead of giving them responsibility to solve it. So they continued to be unfair to her. Besides, a fight always got her undivided attention.

Her new partner Louis arrived in the middle of the war zone one evening and in despair Bridget asked, 'What can I do?'

Louis had held back since they had got together, thinking, 'I'm the new guy on the block, they're her kids.' However, with her invitation, he welcomed the opportunity to help.

He asked them if they still wanted him to drive them to basketball practice. He knew that they did. He sat them down and told them that they had exactly ten minutes to go into their bedroom and work out how they were going to cooperate and coexist. He told them that they were the only ones involved in the conflict so they were the only ones who could solve the problem. He also told them that he was giving them practice in survival skills for when they were adults. He didn't want them living permanently in a state of war. He told them that in ten minutes they should come out and inform the adults how they were going to resolve their problem, and how they were going to support each other in the future. There was to be no put-downs, no hitting, no ridicule, no teasing and no screaming!

Louis presented their choices: 'If you can't work out the harmony, guys, you'll find my car can't make it to basketball practice. You choose!'

They looked at him and they knew he meant it. They

didn't consider involving their mother – she was not the one who drove them to practice.

The kids made the ten-minute deadline. With a loss staring them in the face, they stuck to the rules they had created. Louis knew exactly what was the most important thing to them so he chose the loss of it as the consequence.

Bridget learned that being unfair wasn't the issue. The issue was simple – war would not be tolerated. The boys would work out how to stop fighting, how to meet each other's needs, or they would forfeit a privilege. They had to know the penalties up front, like going through a red light before learning to drive, and their mother had to deliver. Bridget didn't have to prove she loved her children. They had to prove they loved her.

How should you respond when Lions and Unicorns try to involve you in an argument? Remember that an argument is never about producing better outcomes; it's about who's left standing amid the ruins. You are too intelligent to buy into a war or to take sides – direct the orchestra instead! Listen very carefully to both positions. Listen to each side with respect and support, exploring the possibilities inherent in each idea. Ask those wonderful, open questions of the curious, intelligent mind: What? Why? When? Who? Which? In doing this, you genuinely honour the input of each protagonist and you are likely to create more solutions than either one of them dreamed possible, and you've acknowledged both of them in the process.

You can count on both the Lion and the Unicorn wanting to achieve as much as possible. Give them a chance to discover that together they can go beyond the war, but only if they cooperate with each other and everyone else. Tell them calmly that they need to consider your ideas and needs to get your cooperation. Consensus should be a creative use of resources, producing more than you all believed possible. After a lot of discussion and input from everyone, building on each other's ideas, you will not end up with the impoverished idea of one single dominator.

How can you maintain calm in the blast of war? Pretend you are asking them to pass the salt. You'll get control. Give them recognition when they deserve it. Treat them as significant. Value each input. They begin to trust people who genuinely want to help them. If you're willing to help, they feel safe. You feel safe. You've won the war without firing a shot! By supporting both ideas you may have planted the seed of mutual respect.

It was hard to keep parents working for the school. School meetings were dominated by two successful people trying to obliterate each other's opinion. The new head of school was exposed to the perpetual war at his first meeting. To everyone's amazement, he stopped it cold.

'You two go over there and develop both those approaches. If you need help doing that, come back and ask us.'

The two were so surprised they found themselves off in the corner. Everyone knew there would be no admission of failure. They were back in five minutes with it all worked out. A lot was done for the school after that.

RECOGNITION IS WHAT THEY'RE AFTER — SEE THAT THEY EARN IT

• The Lion and the Unicorn represent the continual struggle to dominate and destroy any opposition. It is competition as its most destructive.

• To prove that they are superior, they believe they have to destroy others' ideas.

• Remember that the purpose of rage is to keep others under control.

• Helping Lions and Unicorns succeed redirects their energy into being constructive. But you need to stop the war right at the beginning.

• When they have resolved the conflicts between them, hold them accountable for developing a team of people who will willingly support them. You are turning loners into leaders. It certainly shows up in the profit column.

• Provide the cooperation and recognition to help them develop social intelligence. In doing so you will personally learn to achieve tranquillity in the face of fury. Lions and Unicorns don't know they are giving you a gift.

• The key to handling Lions and Unicorns is to respond with respect, making it difficult for them to continue their attack.

• Acknowledge their achievements and win their trust.

Mary, Mary, Quite Contrary

(We learn to love those who always

say 'It won't work')

Mary, Mary, quite contrary,
How does your garden grow?
With silver bells and cockle shells,
And pretty maids all in a row.

Mary Contrary has a deep fear of making mistakes, and as a result, is committed to getting it right. Mary says no! to anything new. She would love a predictable world because she is a perfectionist. Throwing her in at the deep end is an act of injustice. She needs time to adjust to new ideas and change. We owe these idea killers a great deal. You are going to stop feeling frustrated with Mary's negative attitude and instead use her talents and learn that her impeccability can help you implement great ideas.

Ian stood there aghast. Everywhere he looked there was chaos: toys, paper, boxes, rags, cars, and a crust of bread dripping with jam, upside down on the floor. Why was he working so hard to come home to this? He roared, he stomped, he felt sick. Once started, he couldn't stop. He felt that if he said it enough, his standards would sink in. He demanded an explanation.

His wife smiled at him and said, 'No, my darling, this is not the city dump, you got here 15 minutes early. Sit down and close your eyes. When you are relaxed, that corner of the room is yours. It needs your impeccable touch.'

Mary Contrary is a detailed perfectionist; any disorder distresses her. She spends endless amounts of time rechecking what she's checked. She resists anything new because it's just more for her to control and she is exhausted already. She is afraid that she will fail. She puts the same amount of effort into symmetry in the linen cupboard as she does into every screw in a bridge. The bridge has greater priority, and this is why we bless perfectionists. However, she treats everything as life-threatening. The thought of a toilet seat left up is cataclysmic. Adverts for new bathrooms never show a toilet seat up, and Mary does everything to meet all standards. She seeks the unattainable – approval from everyone.

She looks for errors first, and that's where she stops. She can discourage you by being judgmental, intolerant and critical, if you take it personally. She thinks she is trying to help you, but instead can leave you feeling that nothing you've done is acceptable, and this can be very damaging to your confidence. She needs your help to bring balance into her life, before she burns out. She needs to learn that there is life after a hair on the bathroom floor. She needs to learn to fix things without creating stress or levelling blame.

Mary is incredibly stressful to live and work with, too. Debris is one thing, but living without breathing is another. It is not her intention to reduce her loved ones to a mummified state but errors leap out at her, making her extremely uncomfortable. She must do something responsible immediately.

Spotting a flaw that can stop something from working is a

wonderful gift. Detailed perfectionists are the reason planes fly, railway signals work and the chips are in the right place. They ordered the right screws, got them in the right place and paid for them, on time! The sad part of all this is that Mary hasn't learned to enjoy mastering this. She carries a permanent burden – worry.

She expects that you will do things exactly as she would do them, but that is impossible. We all work from different data-banks of experience. We aren't anybody else. In not accepting that, dear Mary Contrary lives in constant disappointment. She needs to help you, you need to help her, but it takes more skill if her interaction towards you is punitive. The skill you need is to accept the gift and put no personal energy into the punitive remarks that may accompany it – the tone of voice or look that implies that you are stupid. You're not – that level of detail may not be your skill, or perhaps something else was more important to you.

In learning to help Mary curtail the degrees of absurdity she goes to in her constant rechecking, you may help her recognise when there is no positive return for her effort. Checking and rechecking what she's already checked doesn't leave time or energy for enjoying life.

Doing something right for the first time is cost- and time-effective. Perhaps Mary is doing what you don't like to do, but that doesn't mean you should exploit her. We all need to learn that developing an eye for detail can help us do something properly the first time. It's an important discipline. Ask Mary to assist by checking something critical – she rarely refuses.

If possible, you need to give Mary Contrary an early warning before you change something. Give her time to get used to the idea. Expect her anxiety, but see her criticism as a contribution, not a personal attack. Be comfortable with it. If you are uneasy about change, she takes that as a sign that no-one is in control and it escalates her sense of insecurity. If your attitude is 'If you don't like it, change it', and you do that calmly and systematically, Mary feels more secure.

Anne had put a massive amount of work into the merger. She had researched what impact it would have on jobs in both organisations, and how to keep ongoing production at top efficiency. She'd tested it out in both organisations and felt confident that this format could produce a lot of gain and as little pain as possible during the change. Anne handed the report to the executive director for final approval. It was handed back mutilated by red pen. She was disheartened, but she took one last brave stab to see if she could salvage anything before starting again.

'What did you think of the plan itself?' she asked.

The executive looked at her in amazement. 'Didn't I tell you?' he asked in surprise. 'It's awesome, but I think it needs to be set up differently.'

Always ask what Mary Contrary liked about it first. Ask her how you could improve on it. In any activity, you need new creative solutions and the detail necessary to apply them. Opposite views that are respected produce incredible outcomes. Do your homework when you approach Mary Contrary, but don't go in white-knuckled. That unleashes a mass of anxiety.

Mary is hard on herself as well as being intolerant towards you. She can be very rigid, inflexible and supercritical. You need to learn to be comfortable during the siege – you don't have to experience pain.

Architects were furious with the city council. They didn't like any of the proposals, but were smart enough to come up with what they felt was a reasonable compromise. When their work was torn to shreds by the works committee before it got to council, they started to defend their proposal. They didn't have a chance. Clare, the administrative assistant to the committee, grabbed their elbows in a steel grip, and they found themselves out of breath and outside the room.

They turned to berate Clare. She laughed. 'That committee is a stickler for detail,' she said, 'and if there is the smallest crack in your proposal, they will find it. If you hassle them, they won't be on your side. Give them time to absorb it and they will champion your cause. I guarantee it will be accepted. You'll find them very useful.' And that's exactly what happened.

Although Mary Contrary is only focused on 'Is it watertight?', you don't need to be squashed in the process. When dealing with her, have confidence in your ideas, compassion for her obsession with detail, and flexibility, because they will plug the gaps. Above all, be patient! Expect them to be supercritical. Never argue with Mary Contrary – explore! Be agreeably unstoppable as you show her that it's solvable.

Daniel, a new manager, was coming. They sat back and waited. Naturally, he would want to change everything, but they were ready. The first thing he did was bring up an obvious problem and suggest an obvious solution. One of them said smugly, 'We tried that and it didn't work!'

'What stopped you?' he said. They hadn't expected that.

'We didn't have the resources!' they said, feeling back in control.

'So how do we get the resources?' he said calmly.

The Mary Contrarys tried their usual tack. 'That's not our job,' they protested. 'From now on it is,' Daniel said cheerfully.

And that's how it went. 'How do we make the time? Who do we need to influence? Who knows them? How do we get to them?'

Every time they blocked him, he'd throw it back at them by asking 'How are you going to fix it?' They were beginning to froth at the mouth. The more they frothed, the more tranquil he became. Despite themselves, the solutions mounted up.

Then came the statement they feared most. 'Who is going to do what, by when?'

'We can't,' they chorused.

'Are you telling me that you are incapable of doing your jobs?' Daniel asked calmly. He just sat there, looking interested. It was quite clear – changes would be made, with or without their support!

And that's how they turned the company around. Daniel would run every problem by them. He called them his critical gauntlet committee.

He used their x-ray vision, turning criticism into an asset, and held them responsible for contributing the answers. Every idea was explored until it worked. He was tough about things coming in on time. Tough about measuring, but consistent in acknowledging what they tried. The Mary Contrarys began to feel secure.

'In or out?' Daniel asked. They stayed.

Is it that easy? Only if you recognise that contrariness can be a useful asset. Offer them stability in the face of change, and problems can be solved. With stability comes cooperation and with cooperation comes beneficial change. You can go anywhere with Mary supporting you. You are teaching Mary to be more confident in the change process.

You need compassion for those consumed by the fear they create within themselves. With patience, focus and unflappability, you can work your way through any problem.

When Mary Contrary harangues you over what you consider low priority issues, know that she must have had a hellish day trying to get everything perfect in her universe. She may be playing out the stress of that day – all you have to do is listen. She is really mad at herself. Let the steam roll by and listen with compassion. Focus on how you can reassure and support her, and when she's poured it all out, offer that support.

Is she expecting too much of you? She is, but she is expecting double portions of perfection from herself. Hear it as a cry for help. Your reassurance that you are there for her will give you the peace that you both need.

Ross couldn't believe Nicole had left the car there again. It left no room for him to get his car through the gates. Nicole parked there because it was easier to get the kids and parcels out of the car. He knew that, but it still wasn't right. She knew better! It was up to her to get it right. He didn't even put down his briefcase before he went into harangue her. She stood her ground, listened, then said calmly, 'I'm sorry I did that to you. I'll try not to do it again.'

It wasn't good enough – he wanted a guarantee, and off he went again. Nicole didn't flinch; she didn't ask him to calm down because he didn't want to calm down. Instead, she listened until he had run out of steam. Then she said in a quiet, assured voice, 'I have apologised and I have said I will do my best. What more do you want?'

She was so emotionally balanced, relaxed and clear. She didn't argue. He sighed and apologised for his nagging. He felt secure in her presence. She didn't get rattled.

Once you don't take her criticism personally, you will learn to value the way Mary Contrary does things – impeccably! It's her attempt to protect herself and us from error. Learn to negotiate gently with her when her caution reaches the bounds of the ridiculous.

In the early days of their relationship, Scott and Amy came into serious conflict. For Amy, being on time meant being half an hour early. Scott tried to be ten minutes early, but from Amy's perspective he was twenty minutes late. She couldn't bear the stress of waiting for him; she became very angry and used up his spare ten minutes in verbal abuse.

Scott confronted her. Did she want the relationship? Yes! He told her that he was not prepared to sit around for half an hour, except at airports. He could commit to being 10 minutes early, but there would be times when he would be unable to pick up his car and carry it over the roofs of other cars in a traffic jam. They settled on the following plan. Amy promised to believe he was not trying to upset her, and to bring a good book to keep her occupied while waiting. So far, they've had twenty-five good years together. If Amy had continued to be demanding about Scott's timing, or if Scott had walked out, they would have missed each other!

Help her see that creativity and flexibility are not products of a disorganised mind with no discipline. Mary Contrary is a creative thinker's best companion. The combination of 'flair' and 'Let's see if there are any holes in it' can make most things possible. If you meet each other's needs respectfully, you are made for each other.

Love her ability to deal with endless detail. She loves the job of counting paper clips, hamburger buns or doing a reconciliation at tax time. Focusing on a measurable outcome can ease her anxiety; she needs a time frame and she hates loose ends.

Perfectionism is not only about high standards; it is a curse, like the voyage of the Ancient Mariner, never reaching port. You can have the compassion to help Mary land the boat.

> They had been married for ten years. Jackie loved Gary dearly, but he drove her mad. He was so good at all sorts of things, from fixing kid's toys to restoring houses. No job was too big or small – he worked it out. What she couldn't stand was that this kind, generous man always started with, 'No! It can't be done.'
>
> The more Jackie tried to convince him, the more Gary told her why it couldn't work. One miraculous day she realised that all the time he was saying 'No', he was just working out how it could be done. He never refused; he just sounded as if he was refusing.
>
> The frustration was on her side. From that day on, Jackie made her request, then backed off. Gary still followed her around the house, telling her all the things he would have to do and how it wouldn't work, while he did it.
>
> All she had to say, with empathy, was 'I know, dear', while she flicked through magazines on house extensions. She was very good at acknowledging his exceptional achievements.

VALUING THOSE WHO MAKE SURE IT'S RIGHT
• Mary Contrary fears change, so new ideas are treated as chaos-creating conspiracies.

• Mary Contrary needs your help to bring balance into her life before she burns out.

• She is as hard on herself as she is on you. You need to learn to use the criticism in a constructive way and express appreciation for her thoroughness.

• When dealing with Mary Contrary, have confidence in your ideas, compassion for her obsession with detail, and be flexible and patient – you'll get there together.

• Recognise contrariness as an asset and it will work to your advantage.

• Offer stability in the face of change and most obstacles will be overcome.

THE GRAND OLD DUKE
OF YORK

(TRADITION SHOULD BE THE FOUNDATION,

NOT THE STUMBLING BLOCK)

Oh, the grand old Duke of York,
He had ten thousand men;
He marched them up to the top of the hill,
And he marched them down again.

The Grand Old Duke is the custodian of tradition. He is the one who holds everything up because he needs to remind you how he did it in the old days. This can be very frustrating, because he resists change and has a love of detail. He will carry out the task as he was taught to do it long ago. He is the one who insists on the right cutlery and napkins when you are at a barbecue. He is the one who insists on tidying the linen closet, then reading a book. He still hopes to win the approval of his neighbours. The Duke can insist on doing a lot of unnecessary activities, especially when you are under pressure. You are not going to discount him. Instead, you will honour his past experience and his wisdom, give him the detailed tasks he loves to do and get on with what you are doing. Your life will be a lot easier.

They were drowning in the last-minute preparations for their daughter's wedding. Barry told his wife that if her father didn't get out of his way and stop telling him what to do, he'd send him home. His wife bristled. 'Well, if that's the case,' Angela replied, 'you can pack your mother up with him. She's been following me around all day telling me how to do everything. I may kill her.'

It had been the same when they were married and when the children arrived. The 'oldies' thought they were being helpful, sharing the voice of experience, yet the next generation wanted to learn on its own.

These family demands were putting a great strain on their own relationship. Their energy was absorbed by the interference and it was detracting from one of the most important occasions in their life. For each one of them, family was the most important thing. Yet they couldn't get the generations to pull together in harmony.

As Barry and Angela held each other that night when all the guests and relatives had gone, they looked at each other and laughed. They only had two more weddings to get through to survive the grandparents.

Then they felt guilty. 'What if they aren't with us next time?'

Never is it more apparent that each of us needs room to create our own life's experience than in the war of the generations. Your parents and their parents all want to pass on the wisdom of their experience. They get you offside by telling you how to do everything. You resist the telling because it implies that you are inadequate, but there is more to it than that. The Duke doesn't want you to make the same mistakes he did. He also wants to be recognised and valued, not just trotted out on birthdays and special occasions.

The Duke of York will also pounce on any mistakes you make on your learning journey. 'I told you so' is a phrase that screams for recognition, but gets him cut out, even on special occasions.

You feel that he isn't letting you get on with your own life. But he is hurting a great deal. Don't treat him as if age shrivels his capability, memories and experience. For some it does, and it is their right to rest. Not everyone is ready to go. Others want to be active, and resent being pushed aside.

Working on the premise of 'use it or lose it', you can value him, keep him active, learn from him and have him accept that if you don't try things your way you will never reach your full potential.

You don't need to discard older people. He doesn't want to be buried until he's stopped breathing. Many older people are wonderful storytellers – all those pictures hanging on the wall have a story behind them. Ask the Duke to be the family historian and record him on audio or video. Children love to hear stories about you and the rest of their family, and he is great for bedtime. Family history will get teeth brushed faster than anything!

Many older people have no sense of ageing; they still feel as they did years ago.

> Jacob was experiencing some difficulty breathing, so his daughter rushed him to hospital. It proved to be indigestion, but they kept him in overnight to do tests.
>
> In the morning, his daughter arrived, apologising for putting him in a ward. She said she was doing her best to get him a private room. Jacob looked at her and whispered, 'I don't mind being in with other people, but did you have to put me in the old men's ward?'
>
> Jacob was 97 years old but he thought he was 50. The next oldest man in the ward was 69, and acted 97. 'I've got a lot to do,' Jacob said. 'Get me out of here!'

We all want to feel significant. Ask the Duke for advice, then listen, really listen, to the possibilities of what he suggests. Ask him about his most exciting day or most frightening decision or how he learned the hard way. Ask him if there is anything he'd like to do or see or change, or share or learn. Older people can be a rich storehouse of information.

> Sandra had moved to a very large city and had married into a very rigid family where she felt very unwelcome. It seemed as if everything was planned a year in advance. There were lists everywhere that she felt would be adhered to even if the building was burning.
>
> It was expected that Sandra would comply, without question. She would be seen but not heard. Fortunately, she found an ally in Grandfather – he was an outsider, too.
>
> Sandra blessed the day she asked Alan if he wanted to go for a drive. He directed her through the towering buildings of the financial district and disclosed a fort besieged by Indians. Alan's knowledge was remarkable. Through his eyes she learned to see the few remaining remnants of the city's evolution.
>
> As Sandra held Alan's hands when he was dying, he whispered how grateful he was to her for letting him be a tour guide. Tears flooded down her face as she thanked him and promised that his stories would be passed on to his great-grandchildren. He smiled, and went on his final journey.

You need to share what you are learning and why you do things a certain way. You might ask the Duke what he likes about the changes going on around you. Hopefully he will launch into history. Can it really hurt to listen for a while? Expect him to complain: he is frightened – frightened about being useless, frightened about not being able to understand, frightened about being written off as insignificant, terrified about not being able to learn new technology. He is so afraid of looking foolish, and afraid of dying.

In this deluge of fear, older people can be critical, intolerant, judgmental, obnoxious and rigid. Don't be put off by the Duke's abrasive, cranky, superior tone. That's how angry he is at feeling powerless. Remember, some older people experienced the Depression and all of them have lived through at least one world war. They must have something going for them.

Many older people can be terrible bullies. Although the Duke won't admit it, a lot of his bullying comes from envy – he would still like to be the significant authority. You don't have to absorb the criticism he directs at you. When he tells you that you must, should, can't, don't, never ... always hear his desperation. Hear his fear and ignore the 'should'.

Most of our parents were rewarded for being subservient, compliant and loyal. Education, for most of them, was based on control. A quiet class meant a teacher with good control. Nobody looked further to see if the children were quiet because they were interested, learning or comatose! Initiative, in our parents' day, was seen as defiance. The focus was on performing well academically. Good marks plus good control equals a good school.

Thinking through a problem, accepting that there may be more than one answer and being comfortable with different opinions were not on the curriculum. Learning skills to negotiate with others in order to create better solutions and live in greater harmony was not part of the focus.

So some older parents wish they were still in command and that you were still an obedient little kid, but those days are gone. The Duke sees you learning new technologies that he is afraid he wouldn't be able to master, and he is filled with regret and envy.

When he looks at you, you have already travelled light years beyond him. Technology breaks the world into manageable pieces and delivers it to your home, on request. You can access the libraries of the world. You might help him experience some of that.

It will be interesting to see how you feel when your children surpass you, and your grandchildren wonder why you are so illiterate. It will probably happen faster than you think! You won't like wearing the robes of the Grand Old Duke.

Jack's six-year-old granddaughter Eliza was watching him shave.

'Aren't you afraid you'll cut yourself on those fat folds? Why are your teeth so yellow? What happened to your hair? Can you see with your eyebrows over your eyes?'

He tried for a reprieve by suggesting Eliza teach him a computer game. Big mistake! She gave him one chance, then told him he was too old to learn. Jack surprised her the next morning by beating her. He didn't tell her he'd been up half the night practising. He walked lighter that day.

Ask the Duke what he'd like to do. Give him something specific to do. Let him be responsible, and honour his contribution. When he starts a conversation with 'In the old days we ...' or 'We're worried about ...', listen! It might be useful, and it might not. It doesn't have to detract from the way you want to handle things.

You could learn a lot by asking him to look back at his life, at the things you take for granted that he would like to have had. Ask him about what he would like to do again, time wasted, advantages and opportunities missed. Ask him and encourage him to continue learning.

You hope that in the future you don't get treated as if your use-by date is overdue. Don't become impatient when you catch him driving down the centre of the road. When you don't have to punch a clock or catch a plane, it is easy to drive slowly, take in the view, and be Sunday drivers seven days a week. He's earned that right. Think of them as 'L' plate drivers and be a little tolerant.

Treat the Duke gently when he is crabby. Let him know you'd like to help, if asked nicely. Don't patronise him as if he is a child. Although the body is wrinkling, despite the cream, and the hair is thinning, despite the hormones, that doesn't give you the right to treat the ageing as disposable. With any luck, we'll all age. You too will look in the mirror one day and wonder how that happened – and so quickly! Life can swallow us up, and somebody will push Christmases closer together, and that's usually the moment when you look back and wish you'd tried more things instead of swimming in a sea of indecision. You might learn to make more important decisions earlier.

Tempting though it may be, don't just see the Duke as a babysitter, even though he may well love the time he spends with the children. He is coming to terms with the fact that death is inevitable. Friends he played with as a boy are no longer alive. You can help him to reflect, to finally give up self-criticism, to recognise what he has contributed and to become a wisdom dispenser. Treasure him before you lose him – he is the keeper of tradition.

GENERATIONAL CO-EXISTENCE
- The Duke of York clings to the good old days and the good old ways. Honour him by listening to his experience.
- Learn to value the keeper of tradition and help him exist in a rapidly changing world.

• Listen to his advice; he is attempting to pass on the wisdom of his experience and he doesn't want you to make the mistakes he made.

• He is not obsolete – give him a job he can do, such as being family historian or organising the garden shed.

• Remember that the Duke's belligerence stems from his fear of feeling powerless. Encouraging him to keep learning and stay active.

• Don't absorb his criticism; instead hear his desperation and treat him gently.

• Involve the Duke where possible. He has a lot to offer.

THE OLD WOMAN WHO LIVED IN A SHOE

THEY WORK TO EXHAUSTION RIGHT UNDER

YOUR NOSE, SEEKING APPROVAL, THEN

BLAME YOU FOR LETTING THEM DO IT

There was an old woman
Who lived in a shoe.
She had so many children
She didn't know what to do.
She gave them some broth without any bread,
She whipped them all soundly and put them to bed.

The Old Woman in the Shoe feels responsible for the sun rising, the world turning and everybody on it. Busy? You bet she is! She will tell you how exhausted she is, but never let you help her. She will also try to run your life, without invitation. Is she happy? No, she's not! She lives in terror of error. Should you resent her for treating you as incompetent? It has nothing to do with you. She is driven to doing everything for everybody the right way (hers), to never fail, and to do it all yesterday. She is screaming for recognition. Will you give it? No, you won't, because she implies that you are incompetent and makes you feel guilty at the same time. You are going to love her and not leave her, and help her get off her very un-merry-go-round of martyrdom. Then you'll get back to your life.

The barbecue had been a lot of fun, except for one thing. The older brother of the host was trying to organise things. The rest of the crowd wanted to relax and enjoy each other's company.

Julian was about to clear the almost-empty plate of one guest, when he paused in horror. 'Eat your crusts,' he said before he could stop himself.

She looked up at him calmly and smiled, 'I've made a guilt-free decision not to eat my crusts. What guilt-free decisions have you made today?'

Julian froze on the spot. He had never made a guilt-free decision in his life. Such lack of responsibility was the reason the world was chaotic. That was why he worked so hard to put order and predictability into the world. Uncertainty frightened people; Julian was dedicated to stability.

Well, he thought, if she is that irresponsible, she can sit there until the crusts are rock solid. It never occurred to him that it was her right to leave the crusts. The incident continued to haunt him for weeks. He should have emptied the crusts and put them out for the birds, he thought.

The Old Woman is the self-appointed saviour of the world. She is responsible not through choice, but through guilt. She has no idea that she has a right to choose. Instead, she responds to rules from her past, made by other people. She never questions the validity of those rules. She is the rigid, empty shell of the over-compliant.

The Old Woman wants to be appreciated for everything she does. She feels that is her due, but she imposes her rules on you, and you resent her deeply. She does things for you without asking, then tells you how much she's done, to seek your appreciation. If you do acknowledge what she's done, she discounts it. 'It's nothing,' she says, playing the martyr every day.

The Old Woman is rule-driven, so she can be intolerant, judgmental, abrupt, abrasive, sarcastic, cynical and highly critical of everyone. Rules are not meant to add to the joy of being alive – they make her life a misery. Oh, how she nags! She sets standards so high that even she cannot attain them. She is driven, hassled, worried, and she sighs a lot. No matter how much she does, she has no sense of being worthy or lovable. Why would she feel worthy? She abuses herself by discounting what she does, and nothing she does is significant to others.

She resents your freedom to choose and she holds you responsible for the disharmony in the world. Will she let you help? Absolutely not. Her view is that you are incompetent and irresponsible. She doesn't want shared responsibility, because you could mess it up; and she wants full credit for her contribution.

She harbours a deep fear of failure. What if she didn't check something (such as toilet paper) and it came apart or ran out? This dear one expects to anticipate earthquake, flood and bushfire. She will never admit it, but she loves a crisis. It offers her an opportunity to be outstanding. She feels guilty about that, too.

She never questions the role she plays. She never asks, 'Is this my responsibility? Am I taking over? Am I dominating another's right of choice? Am I implying that others are inadequate and incapable of making decisions?' She never thinks about her impact on anyone else at all! She has been known to grab the fork out of your mouth before you've swallowed the last bite. The kitchen looks as if it never has, and never will, experience food preparation. Does she enjoy life? She'd feel guilty if she did!

She is prone to ulcers, headaches and despair, and is often very lonely. She is a perfectionist trying to avoid the possibility that other people will be critical of her. Many Old Women are haunted by the belief that if they didn't continue to do things, we wouldn't care if they existed or not. Doing so much develops competence, but few friends. It doesn't take long before their arrival is seen as an invasion.

Georgia would walk into her friend Lisa's kitchen and immediately start tidying up; it was as though she was a whirling dervish. At first, her friend was grateful. That was all the encouragement she needed, so she started rearranging the cupboards.

When Lisa's husband came home that night he started banging the cupboard doors. 'Where are the glasses?' he shouted in frustration. Lisa felt the despair of inadequacy. Things had been arranged the way her family liked them, even if she was wrong. Now she had allowed Georgia to impose her standards on their life. 'I just rearranged things,' she said, taking the blame.

But Georgia was on a roll. Following on from her success with the glasses, she started to creep systematically over Lisa's entire house – being helpful. When she attacked their bedroom wardrobe while Lisa was making coffee, it was the end.

The next day, when Georgia went to the front door it was locked. She knocked, but there was no answer, even though she knew Lisa was at home.

A close relationship ended because the Old Woman couldn't judge when helpfulness became intrusion. She never learned the wisdom of asking permission or sharing information. She bulldozed ahead. The title of her song was 'Look how helpful I am'. The song Lisa heard was 'I'm more organised than you'.

Lisa did not know where to draw the line on the Old

Woman's intrusion and still maintain the friendship. In fact, she felt smothered for years to come. It was as though she'd been possessed. She went from being open, friendly and welcoming to becoming withdrawn and reserved. Unfinished business can do that.

There are several good reasons for stopping the Old Woman: having a balanced relationship is one, and living stress-free is another! Getting mad with her and avoiding her doesn't help you; it urges her to try harder, showing you how much she's done and why you should be grateful.

A young widow, Beth, with two small children, was introduced to a single man at a dinner party. Everyone around the table was hoping for great things to happen. Sure enough, it wasn't long before they were dating. Although Andrew was an accountant, banging nails was his greatest joy. He was a natural handyman.

At first Beth was thrilled. Every Saturday morning Andrew would arrive with an array of equipment any tradesman would envy. She couldn't believe her luck.

But as the relationship progressed, Beth lost enthusiasm. In fact, she dreaded the sound of Andrew's car arriving. It wasn't long before he didn't knock, he would just burst in when she and the children were having breakfast, barely giving them a wave as he forged ahead on a seek and repair mission. Andrew acted as if Beth's home was his. He would brush by her and happily play building inspector. He would start with critical remarks such as 'Look at this mess!' or 'Don't tell me you've let this happen!', pointing to a chipped spot on the skirting board in the hall. It was said with a terse laugh, which Beth didn't think was funny.

Never once did Andrew seek her input. He was truly happy just being useful. It wasn't long before Beth felt inadequate, incompetent and hopeless. She was losing control of her own home.

It all came to a head when Andrew decided to paint her kitchen.

He arrived very early one morning, swept them away from the breakfast table, and started preparing the walls. 'I'm doing it in bright yellow,' he said with enthusiasm. Beth loved yellow, but she hated Andrew.

She could not believe what happened next. Neither could he. She picked up the paint, and everything else she could carry, and stormed out to his car. She threw it all, with as much venom as she could, onto the back seat. In silence, she emptied her house of his things. The last thing she said to him was, 'This is my house. Don't come back!'

He didn't! But the relationship haunted the two of them. Andrew would say to himself a million times, 'All I did was help!' Beth would mutter 'I should have run him over.'

Over the years, the interaction still dominated their thoughts, but the dialogue had changed. 'Maybe I should have asked her,' Andrew thought. 'Why didn't I tell him just to ask my permission?' Beth moaned.

They didn't know how to work out the rules, together, to serve them both.

You need to tell the Old Woman gently that you like the way you do things. You would welcome suggestions, but you like to be asked. You need to say that if you are not asked, and your methods not considered, you will withdraw. You hope you don't have to do that, because she is willing, hardworking, reliable, committed and thorough. Doing things together is half the fun.

But you also want time to sit and share thoughts as well as deeds. You will need a lot of patience to achieve this because she is guilt-driven, with a great chunk of inadequacy thrown in. It's as if she is cemented to a treadmill.

If you see her assessing a problem, say something like, 'Stop!' or 'Don't even think about it.' Say it gently, lightly, not as if you are on the brink of an international dispute. If you are doing something and she starts to hover, ask her to close her eyes.

> They'd just moved in together. Every time Paul tried to do something, Cindy hovered. She looked worried and critical. Paul put his arms around her and said, 'If you watch what I am doing like that, I'll put a bag over your head. Go and do something for yourself.' It took a while, but Cindy learned to do her own thing without enduring a severe attack of the guilts or feeling rejected. They do a lot of things together, but Paul is good at defining clear boundaries when he wants to be alone. He gives her a dispensation to take care of herself with the words 'On the seventh day He rested.' She is beginning to laugh.

Stop her – lightly, lovingly and firmly. Otherwise, she can wrestle you to the ground and take control.

It's unfair to take her for granted, and it's tempting to get back at her by saying, 'Don't forget the papers in the corner', but treating her as if she is unpaid help is cruel. It can also launch a war. She is skilled at delivering bitter recriminations: 'If you didn't drop the papers, I wouldn't have to pick them up', followed by 'You've made this place a museum, nothing can live in here.' This doesn't achieve happiness for anyone.

Another temptation is to turn resistance into an art form: she fixes, you mess. She is 30 minutes early, you are 30 minutes late.

Point, game, set, match. Fury! Vengeance depletes both of you.

It's important to make the time to discuss expectations so that you can avoid trampling each other's needs. You can help her trade her fear of failure for the joy of believing that if you don't like it, you can change it. You are always in control of choices. You need to tell the Old Woman what you like about her, rather than about what she is doing. You can create precious moments when you enjoy each other's company. You can acknowledge her contribution, but before she seeks your approval. You can help her make a guilt-free decision every day. Graciously thank her for what she contributes and graciously reject her interference if you don't want it. She needs to know that you need the chance to be competent. Help her learn to play. It is a long journey from servitude to feeling comfortable at a round table, but if you care for each other and the boundaries are clear, you'll create a solid relationship.

Danny, a man of twenty, came into the compartment of an intercontinental train and neatly stored his baggage. The T-shirt he was wearing indicated that he was a student, but there was nothing else that was casual about him. He seemed overserious, neat, uptight, proper and very anxious to do the right thing.

Danny left the compartment and stood on the platform just below the window. In the thirty minutes before departure, he went from being neat and in formal control to rampant agitation. He pulled at his hair and looked at his watch every minute. Five minutes before departure, Danny started jumping up and down and waving his arms as if he was pulling in a very heavy fishing net. He did this without making a sound, but his face was tormented.

A well-dressed woman of about forty-five strolled towards

him. The more he waved, the more slowly she walked. Danny was now imitating a giant tidal wave with great sweeps of his arms to one side. He did not yell, but his body was screaming.

His mother arrived with less than a minute to spare. She embraced him. It was more of a vice-like grip, holding him at arm's length. As if she was bestowing a great honour, she gave him the 'continental' kisses, with no contact. Her eyes were hard, and her smile was one of satisfaction. The whistle went. With a lunge, Danny tore himself from her grasp and barely made it through the doors before they closed.

He threw himself into his seat, where he curled up in a foetal position. He remained like that, rigidly drawn into himself, for the next four hours. Later, he told his travelling companions that his mother did not approve of his trip, even though he'd been saving for it for two years.

Danny was only twenty but was already an Old Woman. He had given away precious energy because he felt guilty for taking care of himself. To add to his pain, his mother was a Mary who suffocates little lambs, and he was a helpless lamb. He didn't know how to put limits on his mother. She didn't claw him; she got him to claw himself.

When an Old Woman tries to control Mary who kills lambs, it can have a sad, lifelong impact. It's worth learning to manage both of them. You'll learn lots if they appear together.

THERE IS AN OLD WOMAN WHO NEEDS TIME OFF
• The Old Woman is a long-suffering martyr who does everything herself, yet if you attempt to help her, you will meet with resistance rather than gratitude.
• The Old Woman is guilt-driven, harbours a deep fear of

failure and feels both inadequate and responsible. It's a terrible combination.

• Point out gently that you have a certain way of doing things, but that you would welcome her suggestions. Maintain control of your choices and don't bow to pressure.

• Help her by asking if you can work together. If that doesn't work and she begins to hover around you while you are performing a task, stop her gently but firmly before she takes control.

• Discuss your expectations so that you can avoid offending each other.

• Let her know that if you do something together and you don't like the result, it can be changed.

• Thank her for her assistance before she seeks approval from you. This will help boost her self-esteem. If she seeks approval and you give it, she may not believe you mean it.

ROCK-A-BYE BABY

THE ONES WHO NEED A CHANCE
TO BE REBORN

Rock-a-bye baby
On a tree-top,
When the wind blows
The cradle will rock.

When the bough breaks
The cradle will fall,
And down will come baby,
Cradle and all.

Do you ever wonder what happens to people who live in an environment in which they are permanently criticised, put down or over-protected? If they have no model outside the abuse, they can live from cradle to grave with not much joy. You may call them lazy or cowardly, but that is an injustice. Labelling continues the brutality of the abuser by writing them off as hopeless or stupid. Rock-a-bye-Babies are products of abuse, atrophied, because no matter how they tried, they were given unreachable standards and expectations, never encouraged, never acknowledged and always told they were inadequate.

Many of these Babies are like the inmates of death camps – afraid to move until told to do so. They deserve your deepest compassion and strongest support. Rescuing them just reinforces their feelings of inadequacy. You are going to teach them how to rejoin the living and at the same time extend your own ability to control your life. You are going to help them discover the talents that lie hidden. You are going to help them help themselves.

When Drew was about two years old he slipped on the carpet, fell in a heap and the milk in his cup reupholstered the sofa. The family all laughed because he looked so funny. He loved the attention – and the joyous spray of the milk – so he became the neighbourhood fall guy. Drew wasn't sure when things began to change, but eventually they didn't laugh any more. Instead, they called him 'clumsy', 'hopeless' and 'unreliable'.

Family and friends would introduce him by these labels. Drew laughed along with them, but inside he didn't know how to shake off the labels. He was so sure that he would blow it that he usually did. He had no idea who he was or what he could do. He was afraid to think about it, knowing he would probably mess it up. He drifted, and that made him more afraid. He found himself being overly cautious when he was going down stairs, riding a bike, driving a car. His old car was as scarred as his face.

The scars cut much deeper than the skin, because Drew felt awkward within himself. Secretly, he longed to leave his family and friends and go somewhere where nobody knew him or his nicknames, but he didn't think it would make any difference. He couldn't remember a time when he had got everything 100 per cent right.

He continued to see his old friends. A typical icebreaker at a party was 'Don't let him pour the drinks. You'll wear them.' His friends used their network to send him to jobs that didn't demand too much of him. He accepted the pain without complaint. After all, what if he let them down? And it wasn't as if he had a track record that would be of any value. Drew couldn't take risks. He was afraid that he would find out that there was nothing there within him able to cope with risk.

He was always compared with the rest of the family, who were all successful. His parents were apologetic about him. He knew they felt he had failed, and that hurt him deeply, too.

He married a girl because his friends approved of her – the wrong reason. Drew felt badly about it and his wife resented being the decision maker. He was always looking back on his life, kicking himself because he hadn't made his own choices. It didn't occur to him that he could always choose.

Sitting in front of the fireplace, when the sounds of his 50th birthday party were only echoes, he was surprised when he felt a stream of tears trickling down his face. He wondered what it would be like to want to do something. It made him very, very sad.

Babies in the Cradle live by, and try to live up to, other's expectations, so they know what it's like to feel unsuccessful. They are afraid to listen to the whispering of their inner self because they haven't discovered its treasures. They spend their lives waiting. Waiting for someone to say, 'You should do this!' Waiting for the bough to break, and terrified that they wouldn't know what to do if it did. Some of them feel as if they haven't been born and others feel that they shouldn't have been born.

They apologise for everything, hoping to cut off the expected flow of criticism. In doing so, they devalue who they are and are taken for granted and become depressed.

Do you challenge what 'success' means? We have limited ideas of what success is: being slim, never ageing, having a big bankroll or high status. These social criteria can put pressure on all of us. Toilet-trained at twelve months, a university degree, then a six-figure salary by twenty-two – everybody is proud of us. However, it's when you choose your own path that you are truly successful. Unless you choose to do what you *love* to do, success will elude you. If the joy is in what you are doing, then the commitment is there, too. Committed ones stumble and call it learning. They don't abuse themselves. Instead, they pick themselves up, and have the courage to have another go and see it as exciting. They don't think of mistakes as failure. Learning is your birthright, and that's why you must create your own career. Waiting for direction could get you very lost.

The Babies in the Cradle are highly critical of themselves for their lack of success. They feel guilty, angry and scared. Signals from inside them telling them to 'Choose!' can be terrifying. It's hard to do that when you have had little experience at making your own choices and following through with them. It's hardest of all when you seek other people's approval. Lots of Babies know they avoid choice by running into one crisis after another, complaining all the way hoping someone will resue them. Rescuing them by telling them what to do is an unintentional vote of no confidence, and it only inhibits them more.

Some of them would really like to crawl back into the womb, but then they probably wouldn't choose to be born. Some choose ways to anaesthetise themselves by alcohol and drug abuse so that life will pass them by. Others hope that it will hurry. One Baby who learned he had a terminal illness said, 'Thank God it's nearly over.' His second thought was more hopeful. He said, looking around in amazement, 'I forgot to live it!' Babies experience a lot of sickness because getting sick means being nurtured and time off from other people's expectations.

The last thing they need is for you to ask: 'What are you going to do?' That can bring unintended pressure. Choosing what they want to do is their job, if and when they want to. It's important for you to back off and respect that indecision; at least it is a decision. If you find that frustrating, you need to try to understand why you feel that way. It's not your life; surely one life is enough to manage. Still, there are instances where their indecision screams at you, and they are hoping you'll tell them what to do. Don't leave the decision to them.

> Evelyn was expressing her sadness at her inability to make a decision when her five-year-old granddaughter cut into her dilemma. Looking her grandmother in the eye, she said with mounting concern, 'Well, you'd better decide in a hurry, Grandma. You're so old, you could go to heaven any minute now.'
>
> She stared at her granddaughter in amazement. She also amazed herself; she made a decision and carried it out. The rest of the family looked at each other, wishing they had used a threat from heaven years ago.

The kindest support you can offer is to refuse to rescue anyone who sees a first step as overwhelming.

> Little cousin Tim, aged seven, was coming to stay for two weeks. This was a big deal because he was known to be shy. It wasn't long before Catherine's children were whispering in her ear that he was afraid of doing everything.
>
> The children were entering a contest. They talked Tim into doing an entry. Catherine was short by one stamp by the time she reached Tim. 'Never mind,' she assured him, 'we'll go to the post office'.
>
> When they got there, she gave Tim the correct change for

his stamp. 'Off you go,' she said smiling at him.

The child stared at her in disbelief. 'I can't buy a stamp. I've never bought a stamp. You get it!'

'That's the correct change,' she said, oblivious to his panic. 'Put it on the counter and they will give you the stamp.' She kept smiling at him.

'I don't know how to!' Tim burst into tears.

Catherine had to stop her children from doing it for him as she asked gently, 'Do you want the stamp?'

'Yes, but you get it!' He was getting angry now.

Catherine looked casually at him and told him it was a good day to buy his first stamp. He folded himself into a ball and screamed 'I'm not going to!'

'Okay,' she said calmly and turned on the ignition in the car.

The entire bunch screamed, 'He'll miss the contest!'

She turned off the ignition, sat back and said, 'Off you go!'

She started and stopped the car four times amid accusations of cruelty. The lure of the contest won.

When Tim got back in the car, he was grinning from ear to ear. She grinned back. Before the holiday went by, he had dialled and spoken on the phone to his parents, bought the paper, paid for a chocolate bar and his ticket to a movie, and he got all of them into a theme park.

His parents gave Tim a great welcome on his return home. When they went to pay for the parking ticket, he grabbed the money and said, 'I'll do that'.

'No,' they smiled, 'You're too young. Wait until you grow up a bit.' They meant well, but in an effort not to let him fail, they forgot their job was to help him learn.

How can we help Babies to learn? Look for opportunities to

teach them not to go into the dark shadows of comparison. If they hang their sense of worth on being better, it's only great until somebody better comes along. They need to learn from everybody but acknowledge that their choices are made from within.

Look for their talent. Everyone has talent in some form and it is apparent in the things they do with ease and grace. Babies are cooperative, gentle, non-threatening and nice to be with. People relax around them and open up to be themselves. The world could do with more of these skills.

Don't do things for others that they can learn to do for themselves. Stop and ask yourself: 'Do I really think they are incapable of learning, or are they scared?' It won't help to march up and say 'Don't be scared.' Managing fear is an inside job. It won't help if you embarrass them. When it is appropriate, you can share stories about the times when you failed or were scared and took a risk. In this way you can help a Baby understand that every life is full of scary times, and when you deal with fear, you often discover that the situation is not nearly as difficult as you thought it would be. Your confidence will be in place the next time you encounter an unfamiliar situation. The more you welcome the new, the more you'll take control and trust your choice.

If you hear yourself saying, 'It's faster if I do it myself', recognise that you are accepting the Baby's fear of incompetence, and your impatience is reinforcing this. That's when kindness is unintentional cruelty. Acknowledge respectfully what they do. Never take them for granted. We have a culture that unleashes criticism and forgets to acknowledge what we like about others. Recognition comes when you leave an organisation or at your funeral. It is likely you won't hear your obituary, and frankly, that's poor timing. On the other hand, we don't know how to accept compliments. Compliments get contaminated when they are combined with criticism to soften the blow. Not a nutritious filling. We're good at telling people they don't meet our standards, but most of us need practice at acknowledging the things we do appreciate. Unless you have developed the skills of looking for what people do well, how are you even going to put the right person in the right place at the right time?

Students in a communication module were given an assignment to be conducted in groups of three. Each one had to pay an authentic compliment to a complete stranger then continue to walk on by with no other interaction. They had to do this, individually, three times.

While one student paid the compliment, another would record how the compliment was given, then the third would record its impact on the person receiving the compliment. They had to document the process and write it up drawing on communication theory. The students thought it was absurd, that it could lead to anything from embarrassment to harassment, and they protested en masse. The lecturer was unmoved by their protestations.

Before the first compliment, the person having to give it was tormented. They were sure they'd land in gaol for accosting a stranger. A few expected to be abused. Some prayed that no-one they knew would see them making an idiot of themselves. Their fear mounted.

The first compliment was usually delivered to an older woman who looked as if she couldn't outrun them. The compliment was delivered in an anxious garbled message with no eye contact, and the person giving the compliment looked as if they were mounting the gallows. As soon as the ordeal was over the student felt enormous relief. What they had feared most did not happen. 'Nothing to it,' each one said, and swaggered with confidence! They became more courageous and more genuine when giving the second and third compliments. They actually looked for something they liked and they spoke with confidence.

What sort of impact did they create on the receivers? Those who received the first garbled message rushed to the nearest shop window to see what was wrong with them. Those who received the second or third compliment smiled graciously – their faces lifted and so did their steps.

What did the students learn? How to be authentic, to look for what's interesting in others and tell them. To develop the ability to acknowledge another human being is of extreme importance. Many of the students practised this exercise as a lifelong skill. They can walk into a tense meeting knowing that they will genuinely acknowledge the capabilities of each person there at the appropriate time. They can walk up and introduce themselves to anybody. Most of all, they learned that if you want respect, you have to also give it.

If you rescue people by solving their problem, you are inviting them to become dependent on you, and you will never have enough hours in your day to look after them.

In this situation, it's easy to slide into arrogance, put-downs and disrespect that's really bullying. It's hard to resist telling others how to do things when you see them floundering, but in doing so you rob them of a chance to develop their own abilities. Telling them what to do and how to do it strengthens their cradle but weakens the bough. (Technical training is different, involving theory and practice. If you are teaching a technical skill such as brain surgery, a lot of training and specific talk is involved.) So tell them. But expect them to add their own value after a few tries. We are human, and humans learn from everything they do. Doing is the door to creativity and confidence.

An important skill is to be able to talk to others as people. If you aren't interested in others they feel your disrespect. Train yourself to be interested in what they do. Ask what they are enjoying, rather than what they are achieving. You are acknowledging their existence, their difference, their value, rather than their status, and you'll get their support forever.

Seeking help is something we all need to do when embarking on a new venture. For those who are low in confidence and self-esteem, curious open-ended questions are the most useful. Explore! 'What are you interested in?' If the response is, 'I don't know!', you could ask them, 'If you had no limitations and the world was yours, what would you be doing?' Why do you think so many people buy lottery tickets? They are where they don't want to be. When they decide to design their own career and market themselves to someone who is willing to pay them to do what they love to do they will have won more than a lottery – they'll have won their life. You can help them reach their dreams.

Steven had always worried about his younger brother. Especially when he had married so young. The newlyweds just bumbled along, going from one crisis to another. Steven was always there for them, and it enraged him. He could hear himself haranguing them, the way his father had done. They sat and listened, then went off and made the same mistakes, with slightly different variations, again and again.

Finally, the day came when he stopped telling them how to live their lives. He felt guilty, but he steeled himself to walk away.

Steven didn't hear from them for a long time, and that

hurt him deeply, for he loved them very much. He didn't know how they were going to manage. He would reach for the phone, dying to know if they were still breathing, but then he would discipline himself to get on with his own life.

When they met again there was a noticeable difference. They were more self-assured. His brother shook his hand. 'Thank you for not being my daddy,' he said. 'We're working it out.' That was the day they started liking each other as friends.

We never seem to hear enough about those whose lives zigzag, who collect a mass of skills and experience along the way. We are happiest when we set and live by our own standards. Respect those who take a different journey. When we honour every moment, we enjoy the journey and we create success.

LEARNING TO LET GO AND LET OTHERS CHOOSE THEIR OWN PATH

• Babies are trying to live up to the expectations of others, and as long as they do, they won't discover who they are and learn to manage their lives.

• Share stories about your risk-taking ventures so that they understand that others have difficult decisions to make too. If it was easy, we'd miss discovering how wonderful we really are.

• Acknowledge their achievements; never take Babies for granted.

• Encourage but don't rescue. They won't see it as kindness but domination.

• Learn to develop the skill of acknowledging another person. To gain respect you need to give it! Babies need this recognition most of all.

• If Babies were real castaways, they'd get a shelter up without a project supervisor. They'd learn a lot from a good storm.
• It is important to draw Babies out of themselves. Ask them open-ended questions such as what, who, why and how, and listen to and value their responses.

LITTLE MISS MUFFET

THE LITTLE HAND THAT WEAVES THE WEB
CAN LEARN TO DEAL WITH SPIDERS

Little Miss Muffet sat on a tuffet,
Eating her curds and whey;
There came a big spider,
Who sat down beside her
And frightened Miss Muffet away.

How can anyone so frightened, so helpless, so inadequate and so incapable be so powerful? Surely Miss Muffet can't be dangerous? Oh, yes she is! She wants us to be responsible for giving her a happy life. She is a guilt manipulator and silent saboteur who controls kind, powerful people without disclosing how powerful she is. That aura of helplessness covers an internal rage. She has chosen to live like a parasite, through the kindness of others, yet she is highly critical of those who protect her. Other people's decisions about what she 'should' do cannot diminish the fear within her. Many lives are tied up tightly in her fragile hands. If she trusted herself and took the risk to run her own life, she would be stronger, safer and able to create her own happiness. People who are self-sufficient and happy believe that all partnerships should be created equal, and surely one set of parents is enough.

Don't underestimate the lengths Miss Muffet will go to to be rescued regularly.

Jan was driving along the road with her two small children on a dark, stormy night. She was driving slowly because visibility was poor. The accident happened in a second, but it felt like a lifetime. She saw a dark form move quickly from between two parked cars and, before she had a chance to brake, a body bounced onto the front of her car. She stopped instantly and watched as the body slid off and disappeared lifelessly off the bonnet of her car.

She screamed to the children to stay in the car as she leaped out. There in the driving rain lay the crumpled body of a man. A passing motorist who had witnessed the accident said he'd call the police and the ambulance. Jan was down on her knees, trying to shelter the moaning man with her coat. It seemed an eternity before help arrived.

A policeman walked over, casually looked down at the man, and politely said, 'Good evening, ma'am. Better put your coat on, it's very cold.'

'I think I've killed him,' Jan cried. 'Aren't you going to look at him?' She was stunned.

'The ambulance will be here in a minute,' he replied, smiling reassurance. Thank God, she thought. But when the ambulance attendants arrived they looked at the man, then greeted the police officers warmly, without examining the victim. Jan felt like Alice in Wonderland.

'Officer,' groaned the man, 'I was walking across the street and this woman sped up and ran me down. Me back's broken, can't feel me legs. I'm paralysed! I'm going to sue!'

The paramedic had laid the stretcher out next to him. 'Good evening Albert,' she said, calling him by his name.

There was no sense of urgency.

'That you, doctor?' cried the injured man. 'I'm paralysed.'

To Jan's dismay, the paramedic said, 'Straighten your legs or we can't get you on the trolley.' The legs straightened out without difficulty. 'Now lift your bottom and swing it over on the trolley.' And he did, with considerable ease.

Jan thought she was going to faint. 'Don't worry, ma'am,' the officer smiled.

Jan heard herself shouting for someone to deal with the tragedy. 'I didn't see him until he hit my windscreen. I was driving slowly!'

The officer interrupted her, 'Of course you were ma'am, or he wouldn't have picked you. You see, on stormy nights this is the way he gets a nice warm bed in hospital – it's better than a park bench. He could make a living as a stunt man.'

Jan was the one who needed the ambulance.

Miss Muffet is dangerous because she appears to be so power-less, yet she wields a great deal of power, all of it destructive. She tries to get you to be responsible for her care, protection and happiness. She loves the security and attention of being a little kid, but she needs a protector beside her that she can control. In remaining a kid, Miss Muffet doesn't learn the wonderful skills that could give her the confidence to see the world as an excit-ing place. She is afraid of everything: being foolish, looking like an idiot, doing or saying the wrong thing, being laughed at, wearing the wrong clothes, being ridiculed or humiliated. Oh yes, and spiders.

She worries a lot about what others think of her, assuming it will be negative, so she immobilises herself and her brain. She can be wistful, sad, fragile, helpless, worried, sullen, sorrowful, pessimistic, suffering, panicky and depressed. Whatever it takes to get you to rescue her. Underneath she is very, very angry. Playing helpless in a rapidly changing world is a precarious choice. She hasn't developed the courage yet to take on life, and the more you rescue her, the more you unintentionally reinforce her belief that she can't make it on her own. The reality is that you can't eat or sleep for her, nor should you decide for her. Most critical of all, you can't make her happy. That's her responsibility. A lot of people believe that loving someone means being responsible for their happiness. People who are afraid to take responsibility for themselves reinforce that belief.

As parents it's easy to believe that our job is to protect our children and make them happy. What we are likely to get from that approach is children who are non-threatening, compliant and low in confidence and, of course, this is not our intention.

> Diane brought her ten-year-old daughter Simone across the street to the birthday party.
>
> 'You'll be all right,' Diane said reassuringly. 'If you're worried, get someone to phone me and I'll be right over to get you.' She knew all the kids from school, yet her mother watched her with concern until the hostess assured her she would keep an eye on her, which she did.
>
> Simone hung back until she was told what to do. She was very timid while playing the games and she made very little eye contact with anybody. The good thing was, they didn't have to phone her mother – she slowly began to join in, and she even laughed!

Your job is to help your children become confident, self-disciplined problem-solvers who like to cooperate with other people, including you. With these skills they can get on with the job of discovering who they can be. It's okay to try different directions.

Some know immediately they want to be plumbers; others need time to explore possibilities, picking choosing, changing. While they are engaged in discovery, the best protection you can provide for your children is to keep them immune from social comparison. There will always be someone around disclosing the prowess of their children in academics, sport or whatever. Children exposed to different environments and encouraged to explore what interests them develop a secure awareness of possibilities.

Teach Miss Muffet to understand the boundaries of safety and why she must respect them. Assure her that you are there as a back-up if she needs you, and watch her get on with learning. One of the rules is that she keeps you informed of her choices, where she is going and for how long. You are never out of the loop. You are the support system, not the enemy.

In this age of electronic home entertainment, some children haven't learned how to amuse themselves on their own. If they are not encouraged to work it out for themselves, a deep sigh, and the words 'I'm bored' may bring a feast of suggestions from you. If you take that responsibility from them they will assume you'll always be there to make them happy. This can inhibit initiative. Children who give their parents responsibility for stimulating them can slip into a Miss Muffet expectation that their parents are responsible for all their woes. Sadly, these parents won't teach their children the basic rule for growth: try it, and if you don't like it, change your mind. It's not likely that you'll be there when they are 93 to deal with their boredom!

Donald was a powerful manager, good at developing the resources of those around him, with the exception of his wife. If she mislaid her keys, she phoned him. She could get through to him in a critical meeting by creating an aura of panic.

He took responsibility for solving all her problems. The more he solved, the more she created. He also allowed himself to seek adult companionship elsewhere. Guilt and public opinion kept him at home with Miss Muffet, but she and Donald missed the opportunity of growing together in an adult relationship. She remained his helpless little kid. She knew it, and instead of using her anger to develop skills and confidence, she kept him busy with a chaos a day.

Anyone this self-absorbed and deliberately unskilled can be very cruel in order to keep control of the happiness provider.

The men had gone to war together, where they forged a very strong bond. Josh had built an equally strong bond with his partner Natalie – she was his other best friend. He could discuss anything he wanted with her, including past pains. She listened and held him close while he worked through his past. It helped him heal himself.

Allan married his childhood sweetheart, who was very dependent on him. Allan called her 'Babe' or 'Little One'. She never stopped blaming him for going to war. He never stopped trying to make it up to her. The fact that he was conscripted was never taken into consideration. Babe could twist Allan's sense of responsibility with just a look.

Josh and Natalie decided to retrace the action taken by his regiment. They asked if Allan and Babe would like to join them. His response to the invitation was very moving. Allan's eyes filled with tears, 'I can't think of anything I would like more than to trace the guys who didn't make it.'

Before they could respond, Babe intervened, 'We're not going. I can think of nothing more boring than an old war. What a waste of money!' Josh looked her straight in the eye and said very gently, 'You don't have to come, Babe'.

That was the last he saw of his friend.

You need to be aware that a Miss Muffet takes but doesn't give. The pattern is predictable – she lurches around helplessly until you ask what she wants. The reply is always the same: 'I don't know'. You offer solutions that she rejects until you suggest something that she really wants. Miss Muffet's favourite phrases include 'I tried that and it didn't work', and 'I can't do that!' They are expressions that hold you responsible for all the problem-solving. Stop providing solutions. Wait until she asks directly for help; don't cave in to her hints. You can help best by believing that she is capable of being capable!

> Simon was vividly describing the insurmountable problem he was facing. His friend Toby was empathetic and asked, 'How are you going to handle it?'
>
> 'I don't know,' Simon said with a deep sigh, hoping for solutions. They didn't come.
>
> 'I'd like to know how you manage it,' Toby said with interest. With that, he patted Simon on the shoulder and walked away. Simon was left wondering whether to be angry, find another source or try something himself.

When she tries to make someone feel guilty, Miss Muffet can be left feeling very insecure. She doesn't know if her victim would choose to be helpful if it weren't for the guilt, and there is always the risk that the victim might choose to walk away from the abuse.

> Jake's mother had raised him by herself – and she never let him forget it. He'd moved out of her home years ago,

without really leaving. Although he was married and had two children, Jake lived next door to his mother. She refused to acknowledge his family, and she expected him to call in morning and night. She suffered from many illnesses and had an attack of something every time he didn't show up.

With his family on one side and his mother on the other, Jake was finally driven to seek counselling. One of the first questions asked by the counsellor was, 'If your mother wasn't related to you, how often would you visit her?'

Jake's answer shocked himself. 'I'd never visit her. I don't like her!' He couldn't believe he'd said it. It was a shattering admission for Jake, and he smothered himself in greater guilt for some time.

But the truth had changed him. He began to see that either his presence had incredible healing powers over his mother's health or she was holding him captive by illnesses that came suddenly and vanished as quickly once he met her needs.

That's when he took control. He went to his mother and said 'The next time you see me come through that door you'll know it's because I want to see you, not because you demand it.'

His mother grasped her throat and appeared to be choking. Instead of rushing to her side Jake said gently, 'There is a family next door who need a granny. We hope you'll come and see us.' He walked out.

And she actually did, carrying two large teddy bears and an anxious face. He had to escort her back over the fence a few times, but she learned quickly. Her health took a turn for the better.

You can't guess what other people want; you have to ask them.

If you try to guess what Miss Muffet wants, it can leave you open to abuse for not being an accurate mind-reader. You will be blamed for not being able to guess correctly. You need to be very clear: you are available only when there is a reciprocal, respectful relationship and Miss Muffet chooses to work out any problems with you. She has to ask for your help and you have to hold her accountable to doing so. Holding you prisoner to her demands threatens your rights as a person.

Emotional intelligence develops as you deal with your problems in relationships. The more you do, the more quickly you have the confidence to bounce back when you are confronted. If you don't take control and give yourself time to sort out what's happening, what you want to change and how you're going to do it, you'll be confused and feel powerless when someone is trying to control your life.

These skills are critical at work, too. If someone's job satisfaction comes from complaining, don't let them get away with it. It's taking a pay cheque under false pretences. Some managers think they are responsible for making their staff happy. Staff are never to be abused but *they* are responsible for contributing appropriate solutions to make themselves happy.

Peter was complaining about why he couldn't do the job – it was everybody else's fault.

Michael, his new supervisor asked, 'Are you saying that this job is beyond you?' It was a simple statement, not an attack. It shocked Peter. Where was the hand of comfort, the understanding, the kindly rescue, the range of choices? Before Peter could respond, Michael added, 'I hope you decide to work it out, you're a nice person, but I have no evidence that you can or want to manage your job. If you don't take responsibility for, and star in your own career, you may be left with something others want to give you.'

Peter was stunned. Michael had treated him like a good friend, offering support. For the first time in his life, Peter wondered if there was really anything he wanted to do? He thought he should think about it.

In the work setting, some people try to avoid responsibility by acting out both helplessness and victimisation.

Whenever Deborah didn't like the job she was doing, she asked for help, and the men helped her out by doing her work. When she didn't seem interested in learning, the men started to question why they had to stop and rescue her. It divided the office into those who were for Deborah and those who were against. Her defenders protected her, and she felt safe – she loved it. Whenever something was asked of her that she didn't like, she would summon her champions, who accused management of victimising Deborah. It didn't do a lot for their careers.

At about that time, another woman, Kate, who was young and inexperienced, joined the team. Deborah dragged her into the washroom and filled her with stories of victimisation. The newcomer smiled and said, 'I survived four brothers. I'm used to holding my own.' And she did.

No matter who wanted to protect her, Kate would smile and say, 'I'm fine, thanks'. When 'the Boys' took swipes at her gender, she would smile calmly and bring the focus back to the issue at hand. As she didn't react, they stopped. Kate contributed openly and comfortably, asking questions without attacking and staying until she fully understood. She was cooperative and pro-active. In no time, she had surpassed her older colleague, who ran to her protectors. They screamed

'Victimisation!'

Kate marched Deborah into the washroom and said gently, 'I think you've hurt yourself terribly by pretending to be incompetent. I know you are smarter than that. We don't have to create a gender war. We can choose to excel in our own right. Every one in the world has to do that if they want to secure employment and enjoy it. I'll support you and I'd like your support, but I can't do that if you choose to be incapable.'

It took a lot of soul-searching, but slowly, for the first time, Deborah received recognition. She decided to become competent.

Another tactic Miss Muffet uses is silence. In a group, she sits and stares. It's easy for you to feel embarrassed when there is no response, and if you provide over-explanations, everybody switches off. Learn to put the responsibility where it belongs – on Miss Muffet!

It was a class exploring career choices. Stuart, the man conducting the course, smiled and said, 'Good morning'. There was no response; their eyes were downcast, the silence heavy. Instead of ignoring their resistance, Stuart brought it into the open.

'If you use silence as a response, you are putting yourself at risk. People who don't contribute are passed around like dead cats. I don't want that to happen to you. My job is to help you discover who you are and what you like to do. It is also my job to help you learn to trust your ability, to think and to intelligently influence the world around you.

'But you have to choose. If you want to go through life as an observer, this class is not for you. You are stronger and happier when you are doing the things you love to do, and other people are happy to pay you for doing it. If you drift, you dishonour yourself and you may have to swallow what others decide to give you. You may blame others, but you are not making choices and are not committed to making it happen.

'I'm going to put you into groups. Your task is to believe that you have no limitations at all: you have money, age, education, experience and the perfect location. What could you be doing? If the answer is "nothing", pull out of this course and leave the taxpayers more money to invest in someone who is ready to work with their interests and their talents. Let me know what you decide.'

He broke them into groups, and the noise of their chatter was deafening. He was pleased – it was a good beginning.

Take control of your life, feeling comfortable to change your mind and try different things. The greatest gift you can give anybody is to assume that they can learn. Share information, but leave them the choice. Be loving, but not enough to rescue those who don't need it.

A family of magpies landed on the bird feeder. The baby bird was making pitiful calls for food. The parents took turns shoving seeds into the wailing mouth. It wasn't fast enough. The baby bird shrieked between gulps. It seemed to be insatiable. When the parents began to take one seed out of five for themselves, the wailing shifted to rage. The parents didn't seem to notice – they started eating two, then three seeds out of five. The baby bird wailed its disapproval.

Suddenly, the parents flew into a large tree, landing where the youngster couldn't see them. The baby bird stopped shrieking; it seemed torn between food or flight. The food won. The bird teetered precariously on the rim, its wings like windmills as it tried to steady itself on the bowl. Its first attempt wasn't successful. It lost its balance and landed in the bowl, seeds flying everywhere.

The parents watched intently, but did not move. The baby bird did not cry. Instead, it kept trying. It wasn't until it was successful at getting most of the seeds into its mouth that the parents returned. The wail of helplessness sounded again, between gobbles. The parents fed themselves and totally ignored their chick, flying away again. This training was repeated until their offspring simply got on with feeding itself. When it was satisfied, it went to look for them.

Life is uncertain, and when you deal with pain, disappointment or a day that is upside down, you get stronger. You can help Miss Muffet discover that life is a gift to use. You are unjust if you prove your competence by assuming she hasn't the potential to use the gift.

MAKE IT A HABIT TO NOTICE THE ABILITIES OF THOSE AROUND YOU. DISCOVER THAT YOU ARE IN THE LAND OF PLENTY
- Miss Muffet is afraid of failure and entangles the competent in her web.
- Miss Muffet tries to get everyone else to be responsible for her care, protection and happiness.
- Never try to guess what is wrong. Explain to Miss Muffet that you expect her to work out problems with you.
- Wait until Miss Muffet asks for help; don't cave in to her hints.
- The best way to help Miss Muffet is to believe that she

is capable. Look for the evidence. You'll feel more secure if you audit her capabilities when she isn't playing Miss Muffet.

• Help Miss Muffet take control and solve the problem herself by being curious about how she'll manage it.

• The more problem-solving Miss Muffet does, the greater her confidence will be. Partnerships between equals who choose to work together have a lot of potential.

LITTLE BO-PEEP

(RESCUE HER AND YOU COULD BECOME

ONE OF HER SHEEP)

Little Bo-Peep has lost her sheep,
And doesn't know where to find them;
Leave them alone and they'll come home,
Wagging their tails behind them.

Bo-Peep is a manipulator who 'plays sadness' right under your feet. You may ask her, 'What's wrong?' but she turns her head away and says, 'Nothing'. Unfortunately, it doesn't end there, but it should. Most of us are kind, decent people who feel drawn to support Bo-Peep, to help her become happy. If you take on that responsibility, she will expect you to guess whether it's sheep, a new car or a glass of water that she wants. She will also tell you how inadequate you are for not guessing what's missing. It's a relationship with very little disclosure and little contribution on one side. You can find yourself doing all the work, dragging out the information and being wrong most of the time. The issue is not about lost sheep. Bo-Peep seeks attention. It's about 'Prove that you love me by guessing why I'm sad'. She also wants you to guess what she wants and tell her what to do so that you can be responsible if it doesn't work. You can feel very resentful, guilty and exhausted if you don't set the lines of responsibility very clearly so that Bo-Peep can deal with the difficulties she encounters. Bo-Peep wants to be nurtured, protected and parented by you. She needs to put all that energy into protecting her sheep.

They had been together for ten years. Amy loved Callum so much, yet she felt so inadequate because she couldn't seem to make him happy. He would sit in a room with her, staring at the floor and looking as if he'd lost his job and had a terminal disease and was watching the house burn to the ground.

'What's wrong, darling?' Amy would ask, even though she knew what his response would be. 'Nothing,' Callum would reply in a tone of deep sorrow.

If she moved out of the room, he would follow her like a lost puppy. This could go on for days. If she didn't enquire how he was, he would gently imply that she cared very little about him. She would protest, giving endless examples. He wouldn't accept them; they were never enough.

Amy always waited for the aftermath. It wasn't long before Callum would refer to his time of sadness and say that she didn't have enough sensitivity to know what he was going through. He never told her what he was going through. His assumption was that if she really loved him, she would have known what was missing.

Amy always took on responsibility for Callum's happiness and the guilt that went with it. Sometimes she would shout in frustration that she wasn't a mind-reader. She didn't do it very often, though, because he became reclusive for an even longer period of time.

When they made love, it was a time of great joy, and Amy's hopes rose to great heights. Moments later, he would turn his back on her, as if she didn't exist. She felt lonelier with him than when she was alone.

After ten years of trying to assure him of her love, Amy left the relationship, and Callum told everyone it was because she didn't care enough to work at the marriage. Amy never stopped asking herself why she had failed when she had tried so hard to reach him, and to care for him. She never escaped the deep feeling of guilt that she had abandoned a helpless person.

It never occurred to Amy to ask Callum for some evidence that *he* loved *her*. He never gave – he only took.

Bo-Peep wants a permanent parent. Sorrow and silence got her a lot of nurturing as a child, so sorrow and silence are her tools of manipulation as an adult. Bo-Peep always attracts caring, concerned and helpful people who try to make her happy.

Choosing to be a permanent child doesn't develop a lot of skill and confidence. It's a scary world if we aren't skilled. So like most manipulations, Bo-Peep's manipulative gain is also her pain. The nurturing and attention is nice, but Bo-Peep continues to be wrapped in fear. Fear of failure. Fear of being abandoned.

Refusing to grow up has a lot of drawbacks. If we're confident, we welcome the challenges. If we're wearing the façade of Bo-Peep, they are overwhelming.

Bo-Peep sends out wordless distress signals. You are drawn to her pain and her remoteness, instinctively reaching out to help. You try so hard to get her out of a dilemma without knowing what it is. She won't tell you what the problem is or what she wants. You are scratching around in the dark, trying to be helpful. Bo-Peep silently rejects every suggestion, withdrawing into her reclusive world until you come up with the one suggestion she wanted in the first place. You are manoeuvred into telling her what she wants to hear or what she wants to do! If someone tells her what to do, then the blame belongs to the rescuer if the suggestion fails. Does Bo-Peep fail? Yes. In fact, miserably. How else can she continue to control you?

Your suggestions come from your experiences. What experience does Bo-Peep have of trusting herself to solve difficult situations? We all learn by trusting our judgment and daring to make things happen. That's the route to building skills, and skills create confidence.

Bo-Peep is not dumb, not inadequate, not incapable of making a decision. But she doesn't know that yet. If you offer Bo-Peep well-meaning suggestions, you are treating her as inadequate, which puts her in a difficult position. She wants you to tell her what to do, yet she hates you for doing it. Bo-Peep runs on high-octane anger. Don't buy her helpless façade. Bo-Peep really hates to be undervalued. She loves your reassurance, but she doesn't love looking so incapable. Choosing to deny responsibility, she loses self-respect, the respect of others, the joy of believing she can do something, the confidence that is born when she acts and the greater joy that comes in knowing she can.

No matter how much love you pour in, Bo-Peep's bucket of self-worth is riddled with holes. Contributions don't even hit the side as acknowledgments, admiration or love slide straight into the sand below.

Bo-Peep never acknowledges your contributions, yet she exists on your goodwill and support, hoping that you will do the totally impossible to prove how much you care for her. She believes that then she will finally be happy. However, it would not be enough, it can never be enough, because she must take responsibility for her own life to discover and develop her talents. Happiness is trusting and loving who you are.

Bo-Peep initiates very little, has few social contacts, yet constantly expects to be reinforced by other people. Her energy goes into her self-absorbed sorrow, so there is no energy to love or care for someone else.

Bo-Peep won't tolerate her partner having outside interests.

Bo-Peep will see that as a sign that her partner believes her to be inadequate. Bo-Peep chooses to feel rejected, expressing her sadness and pain in silence.

So where does that leave you? Having a relationship with Bo-Peep means there is an aura of mystery around her because of her sadness, moodiness or sullenness. If you accept the impossible task of trying to make her happy, you may have to live on the belief that you have enough love for both of you. But Bo-Peep won't let you succeed because she is afraid that you would lose interest and abandon her. In taking responsibility for the relationship, you will fail, and so will Bo-Peep.

Bo-Peep will resent you for underestimating her and not keeping her number one in importance for every moment of your relationship. Bo-Peep feels very insecure because she can never know if you care for her or are just being kind. She knows there is no guarantee in a relationship glued by guilt. When Bo-Peep appears to be deep in sorrow, ask her if she needs your help. This has to produce a 'yes' or 'no' response. If the response is 'yes', you can then ask how you can help. A 'no' response is clear. She does not need your help. Most times you will have to deal with a 'I don't know' response. This is the moment when you change the rules of control. Ask her to call you when she works out what she wants and walk away calmly. Don't guess what is bothering her. Do not pursue her. Leave her alone. If you choose to be Bo-Peep's mind-reader, not only will you fail, but you will fail her. The guessing game encourages her to be helpless, indecisive and inadequate. She must learn that you are available only on explicit request.

Loving is spontaneous, and is evident in our interactions as joy, respect and our valuing and being interested in each other as individuals. Seeking attention is control and manipulation, not love.

Whatever you do must meet your needs as well as hers. In teaching Bo-Peep to ask, not demand through manipulation, you are asking her to be equally responsible for your relationship. If you continue to give and she continues to take, it's not a good forecast for happiness in the relationship. It's unequal.

Assume that Bo-Peep is capable of identifying what she wants and knowing exactly how to ask for it. Ask her to call you when she is ready to do that. You can be a sounding board but not an advice bureau. If she's not willing to do that, it is time that you nurtured yourself. When you've been victimised by guilt manipulation, you need to remember how to play. If you don't occupy yourself in a healthy pursuit, you are opening your heart to the invasion of doubt. Guilt manipulation does that to you because you are a decent, responsible person who loves caring for others. However, guilt manipulation is abusing your capacity to care. It is exploitative.

In not running to rescue Bo-Peep, you are treating her with respect. The more your interaction with her is on an adult level, the better. You are affirming her adequacy and are treating her as an equal. You are not Bo-Peep's parent. One set of parents is usually enough.

Rebecca had been sitting sadly right under Nathan's feet, as he was watching the evening news. She'd given several sighs. He'd responded to the first one (to which she replied, 'No, it's nothing'). He hadn't responded to the others, ignoring them even when they took on a low moaning tone.

Rebecca began to panic. Maybe he didn't love her. Maybe he was tired of her. Maybe he found her boring. Maybe he just hadn't heard her signals. So she increased the signals, leaning against his leg and sucking her thumb.

She was livid when Nathan got up and went out to the

garage. She could only come to one conclusion – he didn't care any more. She followed him out to the garage, geared to rage.

He looked up at her and smiled. 'Can I help you now?' he asked.

She decided to shut him out once more. 'No,' she signed in deep sorrow. 'It's nothing!'

'Good,' he replied, going on with what he was doing.

Rebecca was furious, and that night as Nathan tried to put his arms around her, she pulled her rigid body to the far side of the bed. He didn't follow her. He said simply, 'The next time you want something from me, just ask!' He was snoring in three minutes.

Rebecca pulled out all the stops over the next few days and directed a lot of fury towards him. He didn't seem to notice. He went on being his normal, friendly self.

It took a while, but Rebecca began to grow up. She got more attention when she played it straight than she did when she was playing 'deep sorrow'. The biggest change of all was that Rebecca and Nathan had more interesting things to share together. Over time, she even discovered she could laugh. It was a miracle day when she first said 'Let's ...'.

The rules are simple: give Bo-Peep one chance to ask for your help. If she shuts you out, accept it. When she tries to fall under your feet in abject despair, step over the body and focus on a positive activity in which you are both interested. Invite her to join you. If she refuses, keep right on with your positive activity unless she asks for something else. Respond positively if it interests you and suggest an alternative if it doesn't. Think through your suggestion before you contribute it. Blend your needs and hers to make it a viable solution for both of you. In doing this, you are rewarding normal interactions as you would in any adult relationship. You are treating Bo-Peep as a real grown-up person.

Silence may mean a need for time out. Real time out is something we all need, and we say so. Reciprocal respect for privacy should be freely available, but privacy should not become an expanding habit.

If a business partnership is important enough to sit down and discuss what you need or expect as individuals, how much more important is a personal relationship? You need to say what you want from each other, and gain reciprocal commitment. You need to decide, individually, what success in living means for you. The security of your relationship lies in the strength of your differences, and in how much you value them in each other.

Paul and Mary were being interviewed separately by the local newspaper. The questions were the same to each of them. They had celebrated their sixtieth wedding anniversary, and said they would love to do it all again.

The paper wanted to know at a time when separation in partnerships seemed to be the norm, how they had created sixty years of growth in their relationship. Their answers were almost the same.

'Has it been a happy relationship?' 'Yes.'

'How did you manage it?'

They said that they had sat down at the beginning of the marriage and each had written down their expectations about love, marriage, finance, children and responsibility. They made a commitment to contribute and support each other. They didn't leave it to chance. They included the right to change your mind.

One of their greatest fears was that they would lose their

individual identity. They wanted to continue growing as individuals, while sharing life together. Neither wanted controlled togetherness or domination to disadvantage them.

As individuals, Paul and Mary expected to see things differently. They decided that listening to each other's opinion was a valuable thing to do. They promised to be truthful to each other. If they wanted to do something differently, they said what they wanted. If they didn't want to go somewhere, they said so, and offered another suggestion. They were comfortable with each doing their own thing. Mostly, they loved to share each other's company, but not all the time.

When the children came, they discussed what they thought their job was as parents. They worked together to teach their children to think for themselves, to support each other and to discover what they liked to do best. Doing chores was not a paid job; it was a contribution. Pocket money was a separate thing to teach them to manage money.

Paul and Mary felt that one of the most important decisions they made as parents was that no child should be compared with another. They enjoyed each other and the focus was not just reserved for the achievement, but the fun of getting there. They made a special effort to share the joys of each day. They encouraged and acknowledged everyone's choices. They were there for each other when things ran amuck, to support, not tell.

The sixty years had rushed by, but always constant was their respect for each other. They were each other's best friend.

Love is a verb; we act it out spontaneously, we share it willingly. It is not given on demand. Attention seeking, and the abusive behaviour that goes with it, has no room in an honest, loving relationship. Every Bo-Peep knows where the sheep are and can work out how to round them up. It's more fun than weaving a web of sorrow.

WANTING TO BE HELPED ACROSS THE STREET EVERY DAY OF YOUR LIFE STUNTS YOUR GROWTH

- Bo-Peep is the manipulator who suffers in silence.
- Pay attention to her before she has a chance to seek attention.
- Teach Bo-Peep that she has to take responsibility, trust her judgment and dare to make things happen. This is the route to building self-esteem and confidence.
- Bo-Peep needs to get back to trusting and loving herself, and being responsible for her life.
- If she tries to make you responsible for her, ask if she needs your help and if the answer is 'yes', go about finding a solution to the problem together. If the answer is no, walk away and find something interesting to do – invite her to join you or come up with another suggestion. Keep doing positive things.
- Give Bo-Peep only one chance to ask for help. If she rejects it, accept that decision.
- Be a sounding board for Bo-Peep's fears and problems, but don't offer advice.
- The more comfortable your interaction is with Bo-Peep, the more you affirm her competency.

OLD MOTHER HUBBARD

Old Mother Hubbard
Went to the cupboard,
To get her poor dog a bone.
But when she got there
The cupboard was bare,
And so the poor dog had none.

Mother Hubbard lurches from one plastic card crisis to another! She operates on instant gratification, expecting to be rescued. Not that she asks directly for help – she hints! She dramatises her latest catastrophe and your human kindness supplies the desired goodies. She never seems to do without because she is good at getting you to feel responsible for her. She takes from you but she also resents you because you are treating her as incapable. Remember, she didn't ask for your assistance! You can honour her by dropping your rescue missions. You can ask, with interest, how she is going to manage her dilemma. In doing this, you are acknowledging her potential and helping her find her own solutions. Only she can walk the journey to herself.

Matthew and Joanna had good jobs. They lived with their two kids in a lovely home, but had difficulty making ends meet. They would career up to the due date on their mortgage, only to discover they were already overdrawn. Luckily, the grandparents on each side never let them down. It became a habit.

One set of grandparents had finally had enough. They were struggling in retirement, but remembering how difficult it was for them when they started, they wanted to support the family.

They offered the young couple a sum of money that they could ill afford. They told Matthew and Joanna it would be the last contribution they could make, and they hoped that it would see them over the crisis and into a secure future.

The couple used the windfall to fly their family across the country for a two-week vacation in a fabulous resort. They forgot the mortgage but, fortunately, the other set of grandparents paid just in time.

Mother Hubbard never learned self-discipline as a child. She took for granted the things her loving parents provided and, as an adult, she still counts on parental finance. Her parents keep giving, and both parties accept that that's the way it is. Mother Hubbard is a skilful, charming sponger who relies on friends as well as her family for support.

She chooses to live beyond her means, operating on instant gratification. Big house, two cars, every appliance. She lives constantly with the stress of barely making it from month to month. She counts on the compassion of caring family and friends who constantly bring bones and other goodies. She is great company and entertains a lot, asking her guests to bring specific things. She knows who is good at pâté or cheesecake. She supplies the knife and fork. It gets her through many a desperate weekend – and restocks the wine rack.

'We can't believe our bad luck, all the bills coming in at once,' she says, blaming bad luck, not poor management, on getting deeper into debt. She is terrified of losing her lifestyle, yet she can't imagine living at a level she can afford, because she has never worked out what she can afford. When friends give up on her, it hurts terribly and she feels deeply embarrassed.

Mother Hubbard is skilled at getting something without actually asking for it. She comments on how bare her cupboard is. Note that she didn't ask you to fill it, but odds are, because you care for her, you will deliver. She takes your offering but resents it because she believes you are belittling her – she did not ask for help! You offer it, she takes it, then negates your generosity by believing you are trying to control her. What she needs is your support, not your generosity!

> Marie began to resent visiting her sister Annabel and her family. She loved them all deeply, but Annabel took for granted that Marie would arrive with the lunch, the wine, the treats and, quite likely, stay on to babysit for free while Annabel and her husband went out for the evening.
>
> Marie would get a lump in her stomach, walking up their drive. It wasn't that they asked her to bring anything but some crisis or other always left them short of cash. It was expected that she would dole out the dollars, almost every weekend. She couldn't afford it, and she was not developing her own social life. She sat in her driveway for a long time before she started out that last weekend. She didn't want to lose the closeness, but something had to change because she felt so resentful.
>
> Marie asked herself how would she handle it if it were a casual friend asking her for lunch, rather than her sister. In answer to the question, she put the lunch back into the fridge, the wine back on the rack, ate a sandwich before she started out and gathered some flowers.
>
> Annabel accepted the flowers with a flat 'Oh!' but she picked up her stride and offered to carry things in from the

car. Marie forced herself to be casual as she said lightly to her sister, 'I thought you asked *me* for lunch?' It was what she would have said to a friend.

'Yes,' said Annabel wandering over to a very empty cupboard. 'But we're a bit short on groceries this week.' It was a statement Marie had heard from her sister for years.

'I can see that,' Marie replied casually, fighting the temptation to rush to the supermarket.

Annabel brightened up. 'Let's go out to lunch,' she said.

Marie had anticipated that. 'Can't afford it,' she replied. Formerly, she would have agreed, and ended up paying the bill. She felt very guilty. What if Annabel really didn't get to eat?

Marie forced herself to relax and focus on topics of joint interest. As soon as the kids started roaring for lunch, Marie excused herself and said she'd call them during the week. Annabel was furious and cool for several weeks. But Marie held on: telephoning, dropping in, having chats and then leaving. She didn't ask them how they were managing, clinging to the belief that they would.

That's the kind of generosity you need to offer – concern, but no rescue. Concern is a kind of generosity that holds a mirror to Mother Hubbard's face without breaking her nose on it. It says sorry about the pain, but implies that Mother Hubbard will work it out.

Count on her to escalate the crises, but don't fall for it, and don't get used. It's abuse. If you don't set limits on her demanding non-demands, you can be moved from the cupboard to a mortgage payment. And non-payable loans, of course. She won't grow up. A caring, generous person can attract a Mother Hubbard. But caring is helping her help herself. As long as you take responsibility for her, you operate essentially with the belief that she can't learn. If she can't deal with her own reality, she will live under the permanent stress of imminent disaster, believing that if she just gets over this crisis, she'll sit down and work it out. She doesn't. The illusion is so great that she goes out and celebrates every rescue. She doesn't learn to be responsible.

Greta was the daughter of a very prominent family, noted for its professional and financial contribution to the community. Greta was noted for her drinking. Every time she got into a scrape, her family rescued her. Greta suspected that they had no respect for her, but were protecting the family name. That made her very angry. She upped their embarrassment.

The family always gathered, united, to discuss her latest chaos. They no longer talked to her; they talked about her as if she wasn't in the room. Greta listened, wondering what she could do for her next adventure. 'They owe me!' She never questioned why they should! She contributed nothing.

At that point, her son Neil intervened. He calmly asked the group to accept that his mother's chosen career was to drink. That shocked everybody, but Neil turned to his mother. 'I don't know what drives you to destruction, but I believe you are the only one who can change it. I hope you do because I love you, but I am personally, never going to cover for you again. I think we are trying to solve a problem that you don't want solved. I think it must be very painful for you to play at being inept, but I have to respect your choice.' With that, Neil left the room.

The family was stunned and Greta was shattered. Neil had ripped the family shroud of secrecy to shreds. Her drinking had never been openly discussed. They referred to it as 'the problem'. They took her rescue to be a lifelong commitment because she was like that. They always rushed in to do damage control.

The following week, in a drunken stupor, Greta drove to a shopping centre and crashed into a sculpture donated by the family. For the first time, her crisis hit the paper. The press had a field day. The family just smiled and said, 'Greta does that sort of thing'. They'd done their homework and formed a committed strategy.

The family held Greta accountable for her actions for the first time in her life. She couldn't pay the damages, she lost her licence and ended up in jail. They all visited her. Greta was surprised that they did. They didn't lecture her; instead, the pleasant conversation was as if they were just sitting around the dinner table. No cheque books surfaced. Greta surprised herself when she laughed, and thought about a career change.

When you love your children so much, it is easy to forget that their job is to leave home, and your job is to help them go willingly and confidently. Leaving home is critical, because at some point, they need to cross the street and you need to let them go with confidence.

Andrew and his father were very close. They shared everything. Like his father, Andrew graduated with top honours in his degree. At thirty-five, Andrew showed no signs of moving out on his own. He was settled, his bed was made, his washing done, there were no bills to pay, no groceries to buy. The lights came on courtesy of his parents. He had a great job and a salary all to himself. Why would he leave? He treated his relationships in a casual manner too: easy come, easy go.

To his parents' hints, Andrew would laugh and reply, 'Give

up the best five-star hotel in town? If you're not shopping at home, you're paying too much!'

It was a terrible shock when his parents gave him two weeks in which to move out. They stopped him grabbing the furniture, his bedroom suite and the spare fridge.

They grieved deeply, for he went without trace. Without speaking to them, he was gone.

Seven years later, Andrew turned up and introduced them to their grandson. 'I hope I'll have enough sense to kick him out, too,' was all he said. He came for a visit, and he came as an adult.

In rescuing Mother Hubbard, you dishonour her. Greet her dilemma with something as simple as, 'Let me know how you fix it'. In doing that, you treat her with respect. Believe that she can learn to manage her own affairs.

If you look around, she seems to manage very well in a state of continual deprivation. Deprivation is the illusion she weaves while living well: TV, video and microwave, and takeaway pizzas are there whenever she wants them. She's got everything she needs to be comfortable.

The cupboard is rarely totally bare. A bit draughty, perhaps, but never to the point where she has to make the hard decision – to take control. She is the only one who can decide: to continue throwing bills in the air to see which lands face up or start learning the rewarding skill of dealing with reality.

Learn to hear her hints. Look Mother Hubbard in the eye and ask directly, 'Are you asking me to supply this?' Reality is on the table – direct, open and honest. She has two responses: yes or no. You are asking her to communicate – honestly, openly and directly. Only then can she develop the courage to take that first step towards self-discipline, self-sufficiency and independence.

When she does, Mother Hubbard will discover that she is capable of financial discipline.

Be aware of the guilt trap and avoid thinking that you have more than she has. Of course you have; you've earned it, saved for it, done without, lived within your means and made priority decisions. It is yours. Mother Hubbard has to learn to achieve that level of freedom and dignity.

You are not helpful if you choose to be her banker. It's easy to dismiss a loan, and let her off the hook. That's giving her the keys to your cupboard. Dependency is not a life; it's a land of illusion and fear.

A counsellor had a most deserving case. Janelle was bringing up three children on her own and the counsellor pulled every string to get them more financial assistance.

One day the counsellor went out of her way to see how the family was progressing. There was a very expensive arrangement of flowers on the table. The woman saw her glance at them and said aggressively, 'I have a right to those. I shouldn't be living in poverty.'

On her way out, the counsellor noticed that one of the kids had an expensive new bike, which he had dropped in the mud. When she commented on how nice it was, the boy replied casually, 'Not bad'.

Janelle believed in her family's right to accept the generosity of the community. She had not learned that joy lies in being responsible for your own life and the direction it takes.

THERE IS SUCH A SENSE OF SECURITY IN KNOWING YOU CAN TAKE CARE OF YOUR LIFE
• Mother Hubbarb never learned self-discipline and thrives on instant gratification.

• Mother Hubbard relies on others for support – emotionally and financially.

• Help her learn to manage; practise 'supportive withdrawal' so that she can discover that she can manage her own affairs.

• Don't attempt to rescue her by doing so you are dishonouring her. She must learn to fend for herself.

• Let her make her own decisions and take control.

• Listen to her hints and respond by asking directly if she wants you to provide something. By doing this you are asking her to communicate with you as an equal and you are holding her accountable for her life.

• Be aware of the guilt trap and remind yourself that you have worked hard to reach your goals, and while you're willing to share, it's a two-way street. Otherwise she'll never learn to achieve this herself.

Old King Cole

NO NEED TO PLAY THE FIDDLE WHEN THE

PLACE IS BURNING DOWN

Old King Cole
Was a merry old soul,
And a merry old soul was he.
He called for his pipe,
And he called for his bowl,
And he called for his fiddlers three.

He is perpetual fun: disarming, charming and always agreeable. He is the life of the party! He promises us everything, yet delivers nothing. Is he reliable? Absolutely not! He is incredibly creative at telling us why he couldn't deliver. But you are going to learn to enjoy him, tap into his creativity and not carry the load for him.

Kay loved Bill dearly. He was such a charming, delightful man. Wherever he was, it was like a party, except that she did all the work.

While Bill entertained a cast of hundreds (heaven knows where he found them, the most casual of acquaintances were invited), Kay ran around, somehow making ends meet and getting the kids attended to. Bill never lifted a hand to help.

He always said he would, but he would get interested in the television or the sports column in the newspaper. So Kay resorted to nagging, which she hated. She didn't trust Bill when he said, 'Honey, I'll take care of it'.

Kay did whatever had to be done, but it was tearing her apart. Bill was so loving, yet such a burden. She lived in constant disappointment, carrying all the responsibility for the relationship and the family. She was a single parent; he was a star visitor.

Talking about it with a close friend, she broke down in tears. It surprised both of them because she always seemed to be happy. 'Maybe it's happening because you hop in and save the day,' said her friend. 'You are organised and efficient, maybe you scare him off. If you hold back, he'll take over.'

Kay thought about this a lot. Bill had invited the neighbourhood for a barbecue. She asked him to cut the grass. 'Sure, I'll take care of it,' he smiled at her.

By the day of the barbecue, the grass was well over their ankles. Kay decided to leave it. The guests made jokes about the lawn mower being rusty and turning the garden into a forest. Bill laughed most of all. She fought the urge to cut the grass for the whole summer season. It looked like a field of waving wheat.

One evening, as they approached their house, they saw that the words CUT ME in letters over a metre long had been mown into their lawn. Bill laughed so hard and stopped the car to enjoy it but Kay didn't laugh. Their place looked like a derelict dump. Every car that passed their home could read it. It became the neighbourhood joke and their children suffered most from the jibes.

The snow finally covered up the message, and in the spring, new shoots did their best to push their way up. The

CUT ME message was still visible, but Kay wasn't. She'd packed up the kids and left just before Christmas. Bill got lots of invitations for dinner. Poor guy! How could she hurt him so badly?

Everyone enjoys King Cole's company, provided you don't live with him, work with him or count on him to contribute. He manages a free ride on every social interaction. You couldn't find a nicer guy. He is affable, approachable, a great storyteller and he knows all the latest jokes. You feel comfortable with him because he creates an atmosphere that is relaxed. That is talent, but he is using it to avoid being responsible.

King Cole has the ability, like any comic, to size up people and situations with considerable accuracy. He has a brilliant memory and is an exceptional communicator and great entertainer with an excellent grasp of detail. He misses nothing, yet this is merely more talent used for hiding.

What does King Cole do with all this talent, beyond being entertaining? Nothing! He has avoided taking responsibility for so long, he has little confidence and no direction. He ducks and weaves his way out of making a decision by creating a façade of merriment to cover his pain. Others lead, he follows, but inside he hates it.

Leisure becomes a full-time occupation without the survival skills or the financial backing to support it. He watches life being lived by others. Television, sports, computer games and the Internet are all filling in time for him.

Is he happy? No. King Cole takes jobs where he thinks he's safe, and he expects his humour to protect him. He doesn't complete tasks because someone is always there to do that for him. When you pick up the pieces and complete the job, it doesn't give King Cole the skill, the confidence or the experience he needs to be responsible. So he drifts from job to job, becoming more afraid of making decisions, of following through and of having an opinion on anything. Being so vulnerable, he chooses to lead a life that is conflict- and failure-free. He fails in order not to fail. He agrees with everyone yet he hates it.

He has very creative ideas and he tests these ideas by asking people what they think. He delivers the idea in the form of a joke, and it is usually taken as a joke. King Cole often has a mind that is beyond most of us, but never the confidence to go with it. If there is a hint of criticism from anybody, he discards his idea as stupid or unworkable, accepting everybody's opinion as superior to his own. He is brutally critical of himself, just as others before have been to him. Someone, somewhere, was once very cruel to this creative kid. He became bitter, twisted and cynical as he grew older, and cynicism is the voice of despair.

In your frustration, you may believe that it's faster to do something yourself, letting him off the hook. In not holding him accountable for delivery, you are telling him that he is hopeless, which perpetuates the tragedy. In a work situation, some of you get to the point of firing King Cole, feeling guilty that you fired the nicest person you'd ever met. But in the end, we must pay for substance, not just charm and enthusiasm.

In a demanding world, King Cole chooses not to grow up. If you cover up for him, it's the worst thing you can do – it's like awarding him first prize in incompetence. It's demoralising and it also reinforces his opinion of himself as worthless. His kids will get very little direction from him, but sometimes the kids can learn a lot from someone avoiding life.

Every time Michael came home from school, the house was in a shambles. He'd heard other parents telling the kids to tidy up when they'd finished playing. In his home, he was the one trying to get some organisation into the place. His parents laughed and said, 'Don't worry about it'. He did worry about it when he couldn't find a clean spoon for the cereal, or the cereal.

Michael was the one who made sure that there was milk in the fridge. He was the one who organised his brothers and sisters. 'I'd like to be just a kid,' he thought.

He didn't appreciate the gifts he'd developed until he went for his first job. He sat waiting for the interview, thinking he hadn't any experience to offer! Then he realised that he was the manager of dysfunctional parents! He knew he differed from his parents. He knew he could deliver and he also had their social skills. Michael had the job in the bag. The interviewers thought he was exceptionally confident for one so young.

So how do you help King Cole discover himself, and help yourself at the same time? Identify the skills he has that he takes for granted. Which ones do you need? Ask for his help in that area and give him a victory. He will come frequently to check if what he is doing meets with your approval. Refrain from telling him how you would do it. If he doesn't deliver, don't complete the task, pay no attention when he blames everybody else for their bad luck: the system, the government, the community, the luck of the draw, or the ones he lives with. He can make 'bad luck' sound so unmanageable. He is used to choosing not to choose.

Stop covering up. Stop picking up the pieces. Stop letting him off the hook. Stop propping him up. All these actions are a direct message to him that you think he is incompetent. Get him to choose what he wants to do. Let him deal with the consequences if he doesn't deliver. In this way, you are assuming he is capable. He is, but he is afraid to complete something and find out that he is either really dumb or really smart. King Cole is aware of his avoidance skills – you are going to turn these skills into assets. With any luck, he will get on and pick up his own pieces, but you must leave the choice to him.

You must not rescue him. Assume that he is going to do it and if he avoids it, throw it back at him – and back, and back, and back. You need the discipline to keep being tough or King Cole will out-wait you. Be gentle and firm with him until he is direct in his refusal to try. If he refuses, ask him what he wants to do instead. If you ignore his incompetence and refuse to rescue him, he may move to the brink of daring to try being responsible. It is when King Cole completes a task that his confidence is born.

Be aware that he nurtures himself by being cynical. He mocks, then sits back in self-righteous judgment. Ask him how he would do it instead. He is full of brilliant ideas. After all, that's what humour is – an act of creation, a way of looking at the familiar in an unfamiliar way. Resist telling him how to do anything. The last thing he needs is advice. He takes another's opinion as sacred although he inwardly mocks it. That may flatter us, but it leaves him in death row.

If he starts telling you why he can't do something, assume he'll work it out and say so. Smile and walk away.

King Cole must know the consequence of avoidance. If you instruct him every step of the way, it won't build his confidence or competence. Better to tell him what you want him to achieve, with what and by when. Competence is a journey of working it out and trying it. Doing and learning is the journey to our self. Self-destruction is looking only at what didn't work, or assuming we should be like others. He can't be us. We are all wondrously different.

Make a concerted effort not to nag – it gives him a good excuse to resist! Nagging is a public flogging. It's an exhibition shouting 'This Person Is An Idiot!' He isn't. You aren't. Ask him what he is enjoying, rather than how things are going. If he says things aren't going well, be interested to know how he is going to fix it, then walk away. That's the greatest affirmation you can give anybody: leaving them to deal with it.

What does walking away achieve? You are acting on the assumption that he is capable. If you are anxious and provide solutions, you are reinforcing his belief that he will fail. If he does fail, you ask him how he is going to fix it. It's the most empowering thing that you can do. Watch that you don't criticise how he did it. He punishes himself enough already.

How can you help King Cole become successful? Ask him to do what he does best. What is King Cole good at? Getting people together. He has a vast network. Ask him to get people together for a serious purpose. It could be anything from organising a Neighbourhood Watch meeting, fund-raising for school or confronting the government. He is excellent at finding out what people think or want. Turn him loose to find out what customers like or dislike about a product or service.

King Cole has the skill to defuse an angry person. He can read people like a road map, knowing what to say and when to say it. That is an incredibly useful skill to possess. The skills for merriment can achieve important results for any community in need of opinion-gathering and answers.

It is King Cole's life. Honour what he chooses.

Roger was a talented, well-educated man, with a wonderful sense of humour. It was a pleasure to be in his company. He was the one who made delightful speeches at birthdays, weddings or when someone was leaving the neighbourhood. He was a great community asset.

Yet he did not fulfil his promise. Roger's work was impeccable, provided someone told him what to do, how to do it and when to do it. He refused every opportunity to learn or grow into a more challenging job. He did not like making decisions or taking responsibility.

Gradually, the simplest task became gigantic. He immobilised himself, finding his way into a job that made no demands on him at all. Roger was so nice that they kept him on, paying him the basic wage and finding jobs with little or no responsibility. He kept the section amused.

Most of his energy went into the past. 'I should have ...' was his catch cry. Waiting for the trauma that never came had turned him into a very old man at fifty. Retirement was his reprieve from life imprisonment.

Roger sat glued to the Internet, storing statistics and tidbits for his next merry outing, sometimes watching the sports channel for 24 hours. Everything changed when his family was involved in a very serious accident. He came out of his stupor, took control and, to everyone's surprise, managed to both care for his family and deal with the entangled litigation that arose. He drew on his network and had the best lawyer in the community at his disposal. The strange thing was, he kept control. He made it all happen, showing creativity and initiative that he and they didn't know he possessed.

They used to call him 'lightweight' or 'party animal'. Now they call him when they want a creative contribution. That is what can happen when King Cole chooses to use his talents.

WHATEVER WE DO, WE ARE LEARNING USEFUL SKILLS. LOOK FOR POSITIVE APPLICATION

• King Cole is the born entertainer who promises everything, yet delivers nothing because beneath the façade he has no confidence or direction.

• You can tap into King Cole's wonderful social skills and use them to everyone's advantage.

• He is brutally critical of himself and fears failure. Hold him accountable to deliver his part of the agreement.

• Help him grow up by giving him a task that matches his natural ability. When his creative skills are put to good use, you'll have helped him create a success story.

LITTLE BOY BLUE

THE WANDERER

Little boy blue, come blow your horn,
The sheep's in the meadow, the cow's in the corn.
Where is the boy who looks after the sheep?
He's under a haystack fast asleep.
Will you wake him? No, not I,
For if I do, he's sure to cry.

This chapter is dedicated to those of you who stay in jobs that make your life hell. You don't want to be there, but you talk yourself out of doing anything about it. It's easy to remain imprisoned in a job if you avoid taking control of your life. If you aren't making plans to change your situation you feel more hopeless every time you talk about it. You are becoming Little Boy Blue.

You may try to get rid of the pressure you are under by dumping abuse on others, but a sarcastic put-down or withering glance won't eradicate your pain, and you'll be written off as a person with a 'bad attitude'. Even worse, you may become difficult to live with, snapping at the family, expecting them to understand your increasing frustration. They don't deserve that and you don't need to add guilt to your internal pain. Living with guilt is not freedom. You are becoming a bully. Your partner may feel rejected and abused, and react with abuse. All of this is counter-abuse, which creates more abuse. A vicious cycle like this won't create the life you want.

Pain is your internal warning mechanism asking you to care for yourself by solving the problem you are avoiding. Avoidance is a self-destruct mechanism. Unless you take control and deal with the situation constructively, you can't hope for internal peace. Neither can your partner or the people you work with.

Managing your career, which takes up one-third of your life, ranks equally with managing your personal relationships. If you avoid taking control of your career, you may spend your working life praying for the weekend to come, buying lottery tickets and hoping to retire at fifty. Lottery tickets have a very low rate of return, but thinking what you'd do if you won the lottery or were in retirement may lead you to the career you need to create now.

If you disappear at work as much as possible, leaving others to carry your load, you will lose credibility and will be seen as a Little Boy Blue. They will also label you as lazy. You aren't. You are a nice person in the wrong place, and you lose more confidence every time you avoid taking control of you life. In an ever-shrinking job market you are putting yourself at risk by allowing your fear to control your life. If you are waiting for the golden handshake, it might be useful to divide the years you intend to live into the amount you intend to receive. You are worth more than that. Staying in the job and not taking responsibility is choosing not to fulfil your promise. You may lose your job. The loss will never equal the emotional stress and grief you are suffering by staying in a soul-destroying job. Set your own criteria for a happy career. It doesn't have to make the world news, or make your family wildly enthusiastic, but it should make you welcome the morning sun. If you have the intelligence to create reasons to avoid solving your problem, you have the intelligence to creatively solve your problem. Don't talk yourself out of it. You will never make a more profitable decision.

You may manipulate others by getting them to tell you what to do and then punishing them if their choice doesn't make you happy. That's bullying! Everyone takes a deep breath when faced with a big decision, but not making a decision is more frightening. The waiting game destroys your belief in yourself and that's self-abuse. You can be so skilled at masking the fear of making decisions that it may take a while before your employers spot your avoidance strategy. Meanwhile, the fear inside grows long and vicious tentacles, even if you are pretending you are in control.

Steven was one of the nicest, most sensitive and aware people you could meet. His CV said that he was well-armed academically and that he moved frequently, always to a higher position. His latest role was as a senior manager in an organisation that needed to handle a lot of sensitive political issues, working to a tight time frame.

From the start, he had difficulty. He was supposed to run the strategic thinking unit so that the executive could frame its policies. Steven contributed nothing. He listened. When they asked for his contribution, he would just smile and say he would contribute once he had fully assessed the situation. A year and a half later, he was still assessing. Other managers pitched in to carry him. Steven never seemed flustered; in fact he always presented as quietly confident, so everyone kept waiting for his revelations. Meanwhile, there was a high staff turnover and pressure on the executive to take action.

Steven left the organisation after two years. It turned out he didn't give his staff information that was critical to their performance, such as dates for project completion. He drew everything to himself, including the mail. Very little came out of his department. He would suddenly be confronted with a deadline he'd overlooked, and direct staff to produce results at the last minute. That left them inadequately prepared, operating on insufficient information, feeling exposed and hating him.

Steven would gently chide his staff for their poor performance. 'You are letting me down,' he said. Yet they had to ask his permission to break for a cup of coffee.

When the executive confronted him, he stared at them in sorrow. He kept asking for more staff because of the workload. They gave him more staff but nothing changed. After he left, someone thought to find out how he'd performed in previous employment. What they learned was that Steven was high in theory and low on application. He would not make a decision. The organisation now talks to all previous employers before hiring.

Some of us know from an early age what we are going to do with our lives. Many of us do not. Our parents want us to be 'successful', and they may play a dominant role in influencing our career choices. If you need time to explore possibilities, well-intentioned hints from your family might be interpreted as 'You're letting us down'. That's guilt manipulation! Friends who are soaring ahead may chip in with 'You should know what you want to do by now'. That's competition! External pressure can build resistance, and act as a demotivator. Choosing to be a Boy Blue is an abandonment of yourself. You are where you choose to be. If you are content there, protect your choice. If you are not happy, it's time to create your own journey.

Comparison in families can be very destructive. Don't buy into suggestions that may influence you to drift into a career in which you have no interest, even if you are capable of doing a good job at it.

Kim joined her family's legal firm. The walls were covered with portraits of family members who'd established a tradition of excellence in every branch of the law. Kim stuck it out as a member of the firm for nine years, and the family felt tradition was secure – until the day she said she was going to become a graphic designer. Kim said the family talked about her in the past tense even at Christmas and she wondered why she had wasted fourteen years denying what she wanted to do most. She has never regretted changing lanes.

Everything you do takes skill. Everything you do is experience. You may need to explore what's out there in the community. While you do that, develop the skill to handle people who say, 'Why don't you try... ?' Be ready to say something like 'It's under control, thanks'. Hold onto your right to take time to investigate what interests you. Refuse to be pressured by a culture that is time-driven and strong in the belief that there is a 'there' where you should be by Friday the 26th of whatever. Don't get discouraged because a bolt of lightning hasn't struck you with a career message. You may need the richness of many experiences. Being who you are lies within you. You'll be surprised when you choose to do what you love to do that your next step – finding someone who is willing to pay you for doing it – is much easier.

It's rarely a straight line to self-discovery, and you don't want to miss the things that interest you. Doing work you enjoy is your priority. Granting yourself the right to move around is another. Wherever you are, learn what you can in every situation and become enthusiastic. Doing an exceptional job, even if you hate it, gets you out the door with a good reference in your pocket. Treating a job like a retirement village does not. It's no fun working or living with someone who is stuck in the wrong place. The kindest thing you can do for yourself is ask the question 'Where would I rather be?' and follow it up by 'How do I get there?' It won't be handed to you on a plate, but when you are doing what interests you, the effort spent is a gift to yourself and you'll enjoy it.

If you stay too long in the wrong place, you may end up believing that your motivation is to make more money, more holidays, shorter hours and of course, a bonus. Taking money under false pretences, while dying inside, is not a healthy choice, and to continue to follow another's choice is despair. The more you resent where you are, the less you gain in experience and confidence. Your life is a black hole. If there is no personal commitment you can make your life hell and pass that feeling on to those who live, work or play with you. The pain of indecision can engulf those close to you while the deepest pain is what you are living inside.

If you are lucky enough to be confronted about your negative attitude, take it as a gift. If your confronter is skilled, they won't rush in to take over your life. In fact, the kindest thing anyone can say to you if you are in the wrong job and miserable about it is 'How can I help you leave?' Instead of throwing you out like a dead cat, they might ask you if you could do anything in the world, what would you like to do? If you had no limitation such as age, education, experience, money or location, what would you be doing? In the absence of someone with that kind of skill and compassion, you may have to ask yourself.

Some Little Boy Blues avoid taking control of their lives by becoming an appendage to a powerful person. If they lose their protector they are like an abandoned little kid with no idea how to survive.

Felicity was beautiful, elegant and gracious. The perfect

partner for an up and coming executive. There seemed to be no limit to his rise until he died suddenly at the age of forty-seven. 'Well, at least Felicity and the children will be well off. They will have nothing to worry about,' his friends and associates said.

But Felicity was not coping. Three years after his death, she was spending more and more time in bed. Her friends kept a steady stream of support for her, but she wasn't getting stronger. The children seemed to be coping well. They were getting on with their lives.

At about that time, Bob, an old friend, came to see her. He was shocked by her appearance. She looked so frail. When he asked what was happening to her, he was dumbfounded at her response. She was angry! She said she had always been protected, and she loved it. Her husband made every decision. He would tell her who to entertain and when, plan the menu, and tell her what dress to wear. Her husband had made her feel successful. 'I never made a single decision,' Felicity said. 'How dare he leave me? I don't know what to do,' she sobbed.

She was equally dumbfounded when Bob looked her calmly in the face and said, 'From where I sit, you have two choices, live or die.' His comment pushed her over the top. 'Tell me what to do!' she screamed. 'How do I begin?'

He asked her what she liked to do best, and Felicity shouted, 'I'm only good at making sandwiches!' To her surprise, he laughed. 'The world loves great sandwiches.' He kissed her forehead, smiled, and left.

The next day, she got out of bed. She now drives around the city in her Mercedes, delivering specially ordered sandwiches. She has never been happier. Her friends assume that her husband couldn't have left her with much.

Life is a continual journey. You don't have to be at a certain stage of your life at any particular time. There is no 'there', there is only now. Comparing your life with that of others can be defeating. Once you realise this, you are taking control and removing the external pressure of well-meaning friends. You won't have to go through the agony of being non-existent. Who knows what you like to do? You do. Be brave. Choose to be happy. You'll like it.

> David's father offered to educate him – provided he became a chef. The rationale was that people always have to eat! His father felt that he had secured his son's future, except that David hated cooking.
>
> David married a woman who loved to entertain and cook. She had a natural flair for interior decoration. They bought an old manor house – a renovator's dream – and moved to the country. Sensible people would have bulldozed it, but he was doing what he'd always wanted to do – renovate and fix the impossible with sheer ingenuity, great flair and very little money. Slowly the home regained its glory. Both of them scrounged the countryside for treasures that nobody else recognised. People almost paid them to cart the stuff away, yet they wished they hadn't been so helpful when they saw what the couple did with those things.
>
> Pippa runs their home as an elegant guesthouse and David could do with a 64-hour day to meet the demands for his talent at creating 'gracious living at a price you can afford'. Oh, and when his parents come to visit, Pippa cooks!

Allowing yourself to be rescued is the worst thing you can do. Rescuers can get very frustrated with constantly carrying you, if no matter what they do, you don't seem to learn. They can reach a limit and hit back; this is often a gift in disguise.

Sean marched up to the banker, brimming with confidence. He was the son of a very wealthy businessman. He wanted several million dollars to start his business and he was furious when the banker asked for collateral.

'Don't you know who I am?' Sean said in amazement, arrogance oozing from every pore.

'I know who your father is,' was the calm reply, 'but I have yet to discover your capabilities.' The would-be client stormed out the door.

It wasn't long before the banker had a call from the father. 'Do I have to remind you about the amount of business I do with the bank?'

The banker asked him if he was going to stand as guarantor for the loan. The father's reply was, 'You know I'd be good for it, if things don't go right, but of course they will.'

The banker stuck to his ground through incredible intimidation, until he was told from 'higher up', to make the loan on the verbal promise of the father.

When Sean was threatened with bankruptcy, his father arrived with an entourage of lawyers and promised to make up the deficit. Everybody relaxed until, as he was going out the door, the father changed his mind and called back, 'No, I won't. Let him sink!'

The issue is still in the courts. The banker offered to help Sean learn from the experience, beginning with Sean defining immediate small goals and assessing what he needed to do to achieve them. The offer was gratefully accepted.

Give up playing Boy Blue and listen to your inner wisdom. What do you want? When you let yourself take that step you'll find many ways to achieve it. When you do, work will become a joy. You'll be liberated from the pain of indecision and avoidance. It's not necessary to take an 'all or nothing approach', which is one of the ways a Boy Blue avoids taking control. The first step can be a combination of hating the job and loving what it pays for.

Jody wanted to fly. Her parents talked her into the secure choice of being an accountant. She hated it, until she found a way to use accountancy to give her enough time and financial freedom to do what she really wanted – fly gliders.

John stuck at a job he hated until he channelled his energy into achieving his dream – photographing everyday objects in a way that made the world rediscover them. His picture of a cow having a conversation with a rusty old tractor makes you want to listen in. Local councils, greeting card companies and the public loved his work. While John was creating his name, the people he worked with were amazed at how he tackled his day job. His attitude turned from avoidance to involvement and he was great to work with. He'd created his door to freedom.

It is your right to discover what you like to do in life and it is your right to change your mind. Don't wait until you retire. Opportunities can present themselves at any stage of your life. Pay attention! You may have to fight the fear within you that can be so demoralising. Fear is self-destructive, unless you use it to follow your heart. If you don't take control of what's happening to you, you can be like Snow White, singing 'Some day my prince will come', from a coffin. A wise person once said, 'Regret is more painful than failure'.

Comparing yourself with others is internal brutality. You aren't anybody else. The greatest joy is in the journey of discovering who you are.

> Jack had written and directed a film that was winning worldwide acclaim. His wife had produced it. They had worked together for over twenty years, scrounging and scraping to stay in the business. An eighty-hour week was the norm. They groaned but they loved it. They had been at rock bottom for so long that they celebrated survival. For them, there was no other choice. Film critics called them an overnight success. Those who knew thought it a long night. They'd earned it.

LITTLE BOY BLUE, COME BLOW YOUR HORN – AND HE DID!

• Nothing stands still. If you don't take an active role in directing your life you may have to put up with leftovers. If you choose to play Little Boy Blue you are living in disappointment, hoping that playing invisible and vulnerable will save you.

• If you are looking for a champion, head for the nearest mirror. There you are!

• Value who you are and the choices you make. Comparison is either internal abuse or an illusion of superiority. Both are life-wasters, and if you stick with them you may lose yourself and the gifts you bring to your life. They are there waiting.

• Love your work and honour your choices. You'll be wonderful to live with.

BAA, BAA, BLACK SHEEP

THE VULNERABILITY OF OVERCOMPLIANCE

Have you any wool?
Yes sir, no sir,
Three bags full.

There is a difference between compliance and cooperation. Compliance is obedience to agreed rules such as red lights or 'thou shall not kill'. Cooperation means that you choose whether or not to contribute your support. It is up to you to choose the level of cooperation you contribute, for it is a gift of your talents, experiences and commitment to support someone else. We only give when the gift is valued and we are treated with respect.

The early authorities in your life, such as parents and teachers, may have thought their job was to teach you compliance. It was, yet their job should have helped you develop a richness of skills that would guide your development as a human being for the rest of your life. For example, simple skills such as walking into a strange environment with the confidence to size up the situation and find out what you need to know; understanding the importance of saying 'no' by offering another solution; and more complex skills such as how to use conflict as a resource to gain the cooperation of others. You needed to be taught how to accept failure as part of the learning process and that if you didn't like something, you could change it without exploiting others. These are just a few of the basic skills we will need if we are going to succeed in any relationship.

If the authority figures you grew up with believed it was their job to protect you and make decisions for you, you will probably see compliance and cooperation as the same thing. If you weren't given opportunities to make choices you may still look for people to tell you what to do. That's a very vulnerable position to be in. Waiting to be told what to do, and the 'right way' to do it, stunts your growth as a unique human being.

If you see compliance and cooperation as one and the same, you may not value your right to care for yourself in the exchange. A lot of bullies will try to intimidate you into complying with their demands. If you cooperate under these conditions the bully believes that he owns you. That is over-compliance. He will see you as a Little Black Sheep looking to belong, and will take over your life, and your life will be unhappy enslavement.

Michael was a kind person. If you needed help you could count on him. Friends didn't think much of his wife, though. Cynthia was very demanding, and Michael never got it right, no matter how hard he tried.

Cynthia wanted the garden path shifted one Saturday morning, and her parting words were 'And for once, get it right'. Michael could never guess how Cynthia wanted anything done because she assumed he would read her mind. He was afraid to ask her because when he'd done so in the past she'd told him to use his head. His difficulty was that his head was not her head. She was famous for telling her world that her burden in life was to be married to an inadequate person.

Michael had already promised to help out two of his neighbours on Saturday. He had given them control over his life by asking, 'When do you want me?' When there was an obvious shortage of available time, Michael told his neighbours how busy he was, yet he still left the decision to them. They wanted his cooperation so they assured them he could manage it, without being interested in what else he had to do. Michael ran back and forth, pleasing nobody. He always felt guilty if he let people down. He didn't even know that his reputation was 'nice but hopeless'. He even felt guilty when he stopped for a cup of coffee, and unconsciously reached for the mug that his wife had given him. It read 'Nice Guys Finish Last'.

Poor Michael kept on trying to please everyone, and remained undervalued, low in confidence and unfaithful to his life. He thought cooperation was one-way giving – dominators and givers.

When you begin to believe that you have the right to solve a problem and to integrate your needs with the needs of others, the gifts you need will emerge.

Shelley was a personal assistant for a top executive in a big organisation. She was good. It wasn't long before the executive said to the rest of his staff, when they were under pressure, 'Give it to my assistant. She'll help.' And Shelley did.

Twenty-three people took that as permission to dump the work they didn't want to do on her. Shelley hated it but she was compliant. They lounged around, talking and laughing, while Shelley did their work. It made her very angry, but every time they gave their work to her, she would ask 'How soon do you want it?' The reply was always 'It's urgent'. Shelley produced remarkable work because she had pride in whatever she did. She kept waiting for recognition and a promotion that reflected her competence, but it never occurred to anyone to get rid of a good thing. They all wanted her to continue carrying the workload.

Instead of saying 'no', Shelley started a 'hint' system to protect herself. It wasn't a pretty sight. She created a moat with a turret of screens around her desk. Still the work came. Still Shelley took it.

Her next strategy was to turn her friendly, open face into a frozen mask, hoping to turn her exploiters away. At first, people approached the turret tentatively, but within a couple of days they simply stood on tiptoe and handed her their work over the top.

Next, Shelley put bullets in her hints. She would snatch the papers out of their hand, like a barracuda, and snarl, 'When do you want it?' 'It's urgent!' They barked back. Shelley was now nasty and compliant. They didn't give her respect. Just more work.

Deep inside, she kept hoping for mercy. Her pride wouldn't let her be less than impeccable, so the work got done, no matter how late she had to stay. Shelley had done nothing to bring about the change she wanted. She was the only thing changing, and not for the best.

One day, over a cup of coffee (she was whingeing as usual), a friend said, 'I hope you take control of your job, you're becoming a nag!' Perhaps for the first time, Shelley asked for help. Her friend became a coach, and Shelley put in a lot of practice.

Here's what she did. First, she removed the turret. Twenty-three people stopped short when they saw her sitting in full view, yet they quickly shifted gears and demanded support, as usual.

Instead of snapping 'When do you want it?' Shelley took the work, looked it over, smiled, and said, 'You can have that by Thursday morning at ten o'clock.' The twenty-three believed that Little Black Sheep did not have the right to refuse and they puffed themselves up in indignation. 'It's urgent,' they said. Shelley expected that, and she never wavered in her tranquillity. Instead, she told them the names of the people who were in the queue ahead of them and calmly said, 'Let me know if you can negotiate with them to give you their place'. They opted for Thursday morning at ten o'clock.

Shelley had made justice a powerful ally! She had learned to teach others to value her cooperation. Had she stopped at her nagging, punitive stage, Shelley would have turned from a decent cooperative person into a bully. She would have lost respect for herself.

By spending much of your life worrying about whether people approve of you, you are giving them the right to pass judgment on you. A lot of bullies will jump at the opportunity to run your life, which means you will live the lonely life of a Little Black Sheep, hoping someone will approve of you. Take the energy you put into worrying about the approval of others into creating a beautiful day for yourself. It's equally logical and far more fun.

He was acknowledged as one of the greatest actors of his time. The world saw him as an incredible success story. He didn't feel successful. Inside he felt afraid, afraid he would fail, and that success would suddenly disappear. He couldn't bear the thought of that, and he became unhappy. He was so afraid of failing that every success brought him more pain.

When the pain was too much, he would hide in a drink or ten. He knew he was destroying himself, but he was trying to obliterate his fear of being exposed as a fraud. He never expected to experience happiness.

One day when he was feeling very low, he said to himself, 'I am an actor. I wonder what it would be like if I were to imagine myself being happy for a whole day?' So he tried it. To his great surprise, he was happy for a whole day. But it only lasted a day, and he dropped back into his black hole, immediately. His pain was excruciating, until it occurred to him that he hadn't given himself permission to make happiness a permanent place in his life.

Being an actor, he also knew the importance of learning to integrate any parts of the character he was playing into his memory, so every morning as he woke up, he gave his mind a command to perform happiness. He started by saying to himself: 'I enjoy every moment. I am creative. I am successful. I am safe.' What he imagined became reality. He expected to be happy, to be a success. He got it, because he believed it.

Both worry and joy are imagined states. If you choose to worry, you throw yourself into a state of perpetual anxiety. Creating joy is up to you. You ensure it by expecting to be heard, respected and valued. Your relationship with others begins when you offer your precious gift of cooperation to others. 'How can I help you?' is the basis of coexistence.

Most people long for someone to offer their cooperation, but it should not be given unconditionally. You should withdraw your cooperation if it is not valued. Tell the person you bring your support on the basis that it is treated with respect. You do others a disservice if you allow them to bully you. Bullies are isolated, and they know you only comply because you are intimidated. They don't respect you and they certainly don't respect themselves. Teach them to make better choices in their relationship with you and they may begin to find that belonging and being appreciated rates much higher than being an outcast.

You are capable of creating alternative ways to solve any problem, as long as you stop suffering in the darkness of over-compliance. You need to train yourself into believing that there are always many possible ways to tackle a situation. There are!

Josh was only six the day he got stuck high up in a tree. He was very scared. A group of anxious adults were circling around the bottom of the tree, tyring to sound calm, while shouting instructions. 'Don't be frightened. Be careful!' Josh clung to the tree like a koala bear.

Tony, who lived down the street, noticed the commotion as he was walking by. There was great relief. Everyone knew Tony did rock climbing and that he would go up and rescue the child. But Tony didn't seem to sense the urgency of the situation at all. He calmly sauntered over to the tree, looked up and said to the child, 'Hi Josh, how are you?'

'I'm stuck,' said Josh in a wee small voice. The adults twitched. Surely Tony could see that the child was terrified. Why didn't he get up there and bring him down? Instead, Tony said, 'A good climber never takes a step until he's worked out at least seven ways to move'. His voice sounded as if he had all day.

'I can't,' said Josh, 'I'm too scared.' 'Then don't move,' was the climber's calm reply. 'Give yourself all the time you need to look around. Don't move until you see seven choices.' Josh started to look around. As he did so, he seemed to relax. He loosened his grip on the tree, and balanced quite comfortably.

'Work it out in your head before you move,' said Tony.

'Combine moves if you want to. Don't move until you see some steps that you'd like to try.'

It became a wonderful adventure. The small, frightened voice gave way to laughter. Tony had given Josh a gift that would last a lifetime. He had taught the child to take control of his life by turning fear into a creative force called possibilities. Josh's courage did the rest.

Overcompliance is not an act of love. It's self-abuse. Good relationships grow between equals: strong, loving, generous human beings who would not disadvantage each other. Relationships like this don't float in on a rainbow. They are created when two people make a commitment to the justice principle and work at it without bruising their differences. They don't keep score on who did what. Score-keeping is based on an expectation that the other person is going to exploit you. A suspicion like that is likely to erode the spirit of cooperation and create a belief that you are on a war footing.

Spontaneous cooperation on both sides is the foundation of love. Love begins with appreciating yourself and the realisation that Little Black Sheep are a very valuable commodity. Anyone who is offered black wool had better be smart enough to value it.

COOPERATION: ONE OF THE WORLD'S GREATEST GIFTS
• Cooperation is a gift, a choice. You have the courage and integrity to be accountable for those choices.
• Compliance supports the laws that are there to keep us all safe.
• Overcompliance is seeking approval and permission. It gives others control of your life. Your choices must add to your happiness as well as to others'.

• If you need approval, it's okay to start by giving it to yourself. Make it a habit to approve of yourself at least twice a day – like brushing your teeth.

• If someone takes you for granted, they need to be shown that your cooperation is not there to be exploited. You are there to help each other.

THE STEADFAST
TIN SOLDIER

BEFORE YOUR SUFFERING ERODES YOUR

CONFIDENCE, HAVE A COFFEE WITH A

TIN SOLDIER

What great waves there were in the gutter
and what a swift current!
The paper boat tossed up and down,
and in the middle of the stream it went so fast
that the tin soldier trembled.
But he remained steadfast ...
looking straight in front of him, shouldering his gun.
HANS CHRISTIAN ANDERSEN'S *THE STEADFAST TIN SOLDIER*

Why is this chapter not about a manipulator? Because to take control of your life, you need to nurture yourself in an environment that is positive and healthy. Staying too long in the presence of predators can contaminate your perspective and thinking. Destructive relationships can consume your energy. Don't allow it. You need to remember that you have many choices. To get things in perspective when you are dealing with manipulators, take time out to restore balance and regain tranquillity. Nurture yourself. If it's okay for you to love others, it's okay to love yourself.

You can learn a lot by spending some time with the Steadfast Tin Soldier. He is everything a manipulator isn't. He is who he is. He deals with what is. He sees unhappiness as a signal to change the situation, so he does, with a minimum of stress. You are about to discover how the Steadfast Tin Soldier faces his fear and gives birth to courage. Every day! He calls it learning.

> Louisa had just lost a dear friend, and her grief poured over. She did not see her little grandson come into the room until he put his arms around her. 'I'll take care of you,' he said bravely, 'until you feel better'.

You know him by his loyalty, and his direct, open, warm and honest communication. When you see him in the distance, his face is alive with joy.

How does he respond to negativity? Well, the Tin Soldier doesn't absorb it. He sees it as someone having a chance to learn something.

He believes life offers many options. He never bothers to think how he can't do something, he thinks about how he can. If he doesn't like something, he changes it, but he is smart enough not to mess up someone else's patch.

The Tin Soldier doesn't put a lot of pressure on himself by being critical. He focuses on the moment. He knows where he is going and gets on with getting there. He frequently changes his mind. He tries lots of roads. He finds life an interesting journey!

The Tin Soldier is glad to have your company, but equally comfortable on his own. He is there to support you, but not to decide for you. He asks himself: how could I possibly know what will make another person happy?

If you are unconscious, you will be in good hands with a Tin Soldier, but if you are wide awake, he would regard telling you what to do as a gross intrusion. He is compassionate enough not to rescue.

He feels great compassion for the person drowning in their own fear, but he's learned that when you decide to decide, your confidence will be sustainable.

There are lots of Steadfast Tin Soldiers, if you look for them. They may not be the most noticeable friends you've got, but they are certainly value for money. They accept you as you are.

The Tin Soldier is the one you ring when you need help to move old junk, drop the pamphlets in letter boxes, announce the Trivia Night or what's happening in Neighbourhood Watch. You go to him to help you with the impossible.

He is the one you trust when you need to pour out your grief; the sounding board you turn to when your relationship is going off the rails. If he finds you getting deeper into pain by reliving it rather than learning from it, he will ask you what you'll be doing when you stop feeling badly. He may even ask if you've chosen a date to learn from your pain and move on to a joyous existence.

The Tin Soldier has learned the wisdom to ask those simple, direct questions that reveal a totally new perspective. Instead of feeling trapped, you start to believe you can regain control of your life.

He will give you time and attention, willingly and lovingly, because he believes that human beings have the right to live a joyous life, doing what they like to do best. He doesn't try to influence your thinking, or knead your personality as if it were a loaf of bread.

He has a deep respect for difference because he thinks a one-answer world would diminish us all.

The Tin Soldier is cooperative. He will shift gears comfortably when change is necessary. He doesn't like anybody trying to make his mind up for him, and he has the integrity to believe that you are capable of knowing what you want, creating it and getting on with your own life.

You may not live in each other's pockets, but you can pick up the thread of your conversation when you meet as if time had not elapsed.

Tin Soldiers are the people who find it a joy to be alive. Every second that comes their way is a gift. *They* decide how to use that precious time.

Luckily, they always have their time management under control, and can always make time to support you. They are the givers, and learning from them will enrich your life. They won't let you become dependent on them, but they will help you discover that your vitality is intact and when you are refreshed, you'll get back to managing the people who are making your life hell.

JACK SPRATT

Jack Spratt
could eat no fat,
his wife could eat no lean,
and so between them both, you see,
they ate the platter clean.

This chapter isn't about manipulators either. It's a composite story of how relationships can move beyond abuse.

The Spratts survived the manipulative wars of competition and deception, and decided to work on building a healthy marriage. Here are some of the steps they took to get there.

In this chapter, you will explore the life cycle of a marriage, from the first stage, when a couple discovers that beyond loving each other, they are incredibly different. If they are to survive conflict, they have to create some rules that ensure that all of their needs are met. Otherwise they will leave themselves open to abuse.

The second stage of the marriage comes with the arrival of children. Both partners want to be loyal to their own upbringing, whether they approved of it or not. This leaves them at risk in their parenting role, when their energy should be directed towards their children, and each other, as they become a family. Stage three begins when the children become independent little people and the parents need to question 'What is my job?

Steve and his wife Paula, both strong-minded individuals, work continuously at developing the wisdom, love and maturity necessary to create a harmonious, rewarding relationship. Their relationship is one that appreciates difference. I thought it might be a good idea to ask them how they do it.

Steve and Craig were born just eleven months apart. Everyone said, 'How wonderful to have two boys so close together!' Except that they fought each other every day, in every way. They competed in school, sports, over girls, and at home they were like wild bulls.

Until Craig was killed in a car crash at the age of twenty-one.

Steve seemed frozen. He said nothing. He showed no emotion, sorting out his brother's things. The family was in shock, and wondered if maybe, deep inside, Steve was glad to be rid of the opposition.

All efforts to discuss the accident were either met by silence, or what appeared to be complete indifference, until some six months after Craig's death. They were all about to eat dinner when Steve began to shake. The shaking dissolved into a depth of anguish. His sobs lasted for what seemed an endless time.

Silence followed. Finally he looked up at them, and in a quiet voice he said, "I never told him that I loved him."'

We are sharing our story because we thought you might like to hear about one couple who worked towards a trusting relationship. We were on the brink of separation when Steve recalled the pain that came with the unexpected death of his brother.

We asked each other: if one of us disappeared tomorrow, would we be glad or sad?

This question shook us quite a bit. We were the very best of friends, yet here we were, arguing over everything. We had withdrawn our respect and our cooperation. We couldn't get a divorce fast enough. We were fortunate that we talked to each other, although it wasn't pretty a lot of the time. We decided to assess our relationship to see if we could find even one shred of the old feeling upon which to build a loving relationship.

We had begun life together with positive expectations, but we didn't share those expectations. We started trying to control each other, both determined to get our own way. Our belief was that if the other one didn't agree or comply, they were wrong. We spent incredible energy trying to straighten each other out. We were at war. We became strangers who didn't trust each other. We had gone from a loving relationship to an abusive one, in private and in public. You wouldn't have wanted to be near us.

We were each other's worst nightmare, deliberately hurting the one we claimed to love. It was unbearably painful for both of us. In order to stop the pain we felt we had a simple choice: separate or stop hurting each other. We sat down together and looked at all the options. We had a lot of friends who had separated or divorced. Even though they were legally no longer tied to each other, they had never separated emotionally.

We had listened to their unfinished business, bitterness, and disappointment from both sides over many months and years. For some, the past never ended. They used up their lives looking backwards. We didn't want to go that route. So we decided to analyse the relationship.

The first question we asked was "What's wrong in our marriage?" It was the wrong question to ask. It disintegrated into blame and counter-blame, arguing from our perceptions of the past. We were on the brink of chaos. We stopped and looked at each other. What did we have worth saving? It was a good question.

We asked each other what were the things we liked that drew us together. We decided to take time out to think about why we chose each other rather than talk about it and get side-tracked. We didn't rush it. We wanted to invest the time because so much was at stake. One of us was ready in half an hour. The other took over a day. It took all the strength and discipline of Steve, who liked to be quick, not to pressure Paula.

That was the first good thing: we realised that a lot of our conflicts arose because one of us wanted to do things immediately, and the other needed time to look at all the angles. It frustrated both of us.

The fast one always took the initiative and loved to 'suck it and see'. There was evidence of big benefits from that approach: confidence, skills and adventure. There were also cases of severe bruising, when the initiator hadn't foreseen the pitfalls. The one who took time had a habit of pouring salt on the wounds of the adventurer: 'I told you so.'

The one who explored all the details hated to take risks. We were like oil and water. One of us wanted to explore the world, to try different things. The other preferred a predictable, consistent life and was resistant to change. That irritated the adventurer, who felt it was a deliberate attempt to clip the wings of a high-flyer who wanted to soar.

That's how we began to use our differences constructively. One of us says 'Let's!' and the other works out how we can. We've developed patience, tolerance and trust for each other's ways of looking at things because we suddenly realised that, in our difference, we complemented each other. We each liked to do what the other wanted to avoid.

In assessing our relationship, we wrote down in detail what we liked, loved or enjoyed about our partner. When we were both ready, we exchanged papers. It was one of the most deeply moving times of our life. There were lots of things we valued about each other that we had never expressed.

We realised that we never talked about the great times. Most of our conversations during the relationship had focused on what we felt was wrong. Both of us had felt deeply bruised. In listening to each other's pain during this session, we'd agreed to listen without blame or justification. Difficult? Yes! Usually, when each of us heard something we didn't agree with, we ceased to listen. Instead, we humiliated each other by discounting the other's pain. This time we deliberately made a commitment to listen, and change didn't occur until we did. It was a wise way to go.

We also discovered that if one of us wanted something, the other should too. That was like believing if one was hungry or tired, the other should be too. If our individual needs weren't considered, we felt rejected. We were living in frustration, disappointment and intolerance. We were in a death struggle with the one we had promised to care for. We were vultures, picking each other apart! We both expected the other to give in, even if they didn't want to do it. Did we explore any other solutions? No. We each took the position, "If you love me, you'll do as I ask!"

The more we looked at it, the more we realised we were putting our relationship on the line over one liking football and the other finding it boring. Most of our life was like that; a war aimed at eliminating the needs of the other. We actually believed we were avoiding conflict. What we were doing was creating a chasm.

We made a commitment to value our right to be different, and to treat each other with respect. We both felt we had to put down some agreed guidelines that would help us achieve this aim. The principles we finally came up with were simple.

• We would recognise, acknowledge and enjoy the good things.
• No attacking. No put-downs. No disrespect.
• We would ask, rather than demand.
• We would listen, and acknowledge each other's needs.
• We would accept that there would be times for togetherness and times for separateness.
• Love didn't mean we both had to watch the movie.
• We would be committed to looking for solutions that met both our needs.
• We would be honest, direct, open and constructive about what we wanted.
• There would be no holding back and blaming later.
• We would accept each other as individuals with different likes and needs.
• We would recognise that equality didn't mean sameness. It meant respecting our differences.
• We would work towards spontaneous cooperation that was fully appreciated, without counting the number of pegs we each used in hanging up the laundry.

Maybe these rules won't suit you, but they served us. We could both make a commitment to them.

Did we have to work at it? Yes, indeed! We needed to accept the reality of another's view of the world. We needed to go beyond describing the problem into solving it in ways that would not disadvantage either of us.

We listen to each other. If the other isn't being under-standing, we called a 'sit down' until we get through. We don't try to tell each other what to do. We are available to explore ideas and we are deeply interested in the outcome. Difference doesn't dominate or threaten our lives. We are becoming each other's best friend.

Have we changed a lot? Yes, and we continue to do so, but not in each other's shadow. We don't cut across each other's development. We started thinking differently, too. When we agree on a goal, instead of arguing over one solution, we now ask ourselves: are we trying to achieve the same goal? If not, how do we support each other's goals? If we both want the same thing, we ask 'What's everything we have to do to get there?' That 'everything' approach saved our marriage. We didn't argue over a single 'right' answer – we used our different experiences to fill the gaps to achieve our goal.

Then we balanced the workload by asking 'Who wants to do what?' The impulsive one of us grabs the jobs with the potential for instant results. The other one takes the more complex problems that need what we decided to call 'Domino Thinking', that is, 'If I do this, how will it affect that?' We learned to use each other's vision. We became consultants to each other. Best of all, we laughed at ourselves and each other without feeling attacked. Out of listening came trust. Out of trust came respect. Out of respect came security, which allowed us to be who we were.

We also maintained our individuality. Now, if we need time out, we say so. We know we can take as much as we need, without pressure. We are conscious of not exploiting that. But because the trust is there, separation does not make us anxious. We get busy doing our own thing, rather than sit-ting around watching the clock and feeling deprived.

The biggest change was when we started a family. We experienced the joy of being parents, but with it, an inexplicable uncertainty. It was some time before we could identify what the uncertainty was. We were no longer kids. That shocked us! Our roles had changed. Not only was there the responsibility for a new life, we were getting older!

That, plus poor sleep and cold meals, produced a shaky time. We were not prepared for the energy and time it took. So much was focused on the kids that we almost lost each other again. We deliberately budgeted time for each other, as simple as walking around the block without the kids. Just us. We got back on an even keel, growing as individuals, choosing to be together.

As the kids grew older and started to compete for our attention, we got shaky again. We both tried to reinvent our own family. We didn't want to have our different approaches to parenting put the relationship in jeopardy, or to mess up our kids. Advice was pouring in from both of our extended families. We listened. We thanked them, but reserved the right to choose what was relevant to us.

We asked ourselves, 'What's the job of being a parent?' We had to go beyond 'brush your teeth' for that one. It took time and patience. And many alterations.

It became more simple as we went along. Given that we didn't expect to come back from the grave to help the kids across the street, and that we weren't going to be in their pockets all their lives, we thought if we could help them be strong, loving, happy individuals who were self-disciplined and willing to cooperate, we would be giving them the foundation to create the life they wanted. We also wanted them to be open, honest, and accountable for the things they said they would do. Or to come up with a better solution. They learned a lot about being creative negotiators.

We didn't want to run the risk of them becoming so compliant that they would jump into a car with a stranger. We didn't want them to be arrogant, self-centred demanding brats either. We came to the conclusion that our job went way beyond 'finish your peas', 'turn down the TV', and 'do your homework'. In fact, it was homework that saved the day.

We realised what homework was for. Teaching the kids self-discipline, time management, and being accountable. It was their job. It was showing what they could do on their own, and it was giving them the skills for the day they left us to build their own lives.

We kicked it around as a family and finally came up with rules that suited everyone.

- Homework was their responsibility.
- They had to keep their marks above 65 per cent.
- If they needed help, we were there to help them think through it. They had to ask for help.
- If they didn't do their homework, or whinged about it, we would supervise them at our convenience. We assured them it would probably be at their inconvenience.

Our children quickly discovered that our convenience wasn't theirs. So they did their homework. It didn't matter if they did it watching TV, with a Walkman in their ears and friends hanging around. We didn't have to move in to control that. There were only two things to be measured: they did their homework, and they kept their marks over 65 per cent. They knew that if they blew that, it was akin to running a red light. Being a democratic group, they could give us a list of things they didn't want to do without, as for the consequence. The sentence of deprivation was followed through. Complaining about it extended the penalty.

Our kids learned to balance their sport, leisure, self-time and time with their friends. And homework, and getting good results. They got to be very good time managers.

We never had to nag.

Mealtimes were wonderful. Everyone got their time to share what was great about their day. They loved getting total attention: one at a time!

Of course we had bad times. We realised how easy it is to get locked into negative thinking. It was hard to resist telling our children 'how to do it'. That would be giving them a signal that we didn't think them capable of solving the problem. We helped them learn how to create a range of solutions, to include the needs of others, and to be strong enough to go it alone if necessary. They knew we would be there for them.

Major decisions called for a family conference, where anyone could challenge anything we were doing by contributing a new solution. We were constantly changing. We must have tried a hundred ways to get equality established, but we did do it.

The method of how to set up a 'fair' schedule to manage the house cleaning, meals and garden was interesting. We tried various systems. The children liked a rotation system. At one conference, the question was asked 'What if I do my area up to standard, and somebody drops their stuff and messes it up?'

A lot of creative thought went into that problem. We all settled on the following rule. The 'messer-upper' got one warning and twenty minutes to pick up their stuff. (They were skilled at synchronising watches.) If they didn't tidy their mess, their goods were considered to be unwanted and the controller of that area could do what they liked with the stuff.

We had a few memorable confiscations. Someone's new basketball boots ended up in the deep freeze in a garbage bag (rinsed out first). Someone somewhere is wearing someone's never worn new blouse. It only took a few imaginative consequences, and self-discipline developed rapidly. We all made the rules. We lived by them. It left more time for talking and enjoying being together.

We are working right now on teaching the kids the discipline of living within their means. Everyone knows how much money we've got, what the basic costs are, and everyone is part of the decision to purchase a major item. Our children are learning that most problems are solvable.

They seem to be creative, flexible and strong. No guarantees, but we believe they will have the strength and courage to withstand group pressure if they don't like what's going on. So far, really good. Nobody has to eat their carrots if they hate them, and we all dish up for ourselves – how can anybody else know how hungry we are, or what we like or don't like to eat? That doesn't mean preparing meals like a cafeteria. We are good at saying what we'd like and don't like, ahead of time, and we do our best to make meals the most enjoyable part of the day.

Resolving conflict is the job of those in conflict. They sort it out without hurting each other verbally or physically. And fast! If they don't, the penalty decider of the week steps in. There are endless ways to do things. Everybody has to work them out for themselves. But expectation without agreement is a scary way to live.

These rules suited us. That's the best thing we did. We often think of the brother who died and bless the gifts that came out of our grief. We never fail to value each other and say so. And the greatest thing of all? We really like each other. We are nice to come home to.

THE GOOD THING ABOUT BEING DIFFERENT IS THAT YOU ARE NEVER STUCK FOR SOLUTIONS

• If you believe you have to prove how right you are, your relationship hasn't a chance. You are setting yourselves up for abuse and counter-abuse.

• Turn an argument into a range of possibilities. Solutions should enrich you both as individuals and as partners.

• You are two families. Use the history of both to create your own pioneering system. Thank the extended family for their input, but reserve your right to choose.

• If you have one extended family member trying to enforce their will on your family, don't argue or defend. Thank them, then move on. The decision to use, adapt or reject their input is yours. It is not necessary to explain your decision.

• Know that people who insist you must accept their way of doing things are probably lonely. Spot what they are good at and ask them to help you learn *those* skills.

• The job of parenting is to create powerful, loving individuals who know they can go a lot further in life if they learn how to create better solutions using their own and other's ideas.

• Children are safer if they are self-disciplined, accountable and confident people who don't see difference as a threat.

Humpty Dumpty

Empowering Yourself

Humpty Dumpty sat on a wall,
Humpty Dumpty had a great fall,
All the king's horses
And all the king's men
Couldn't put humpty together again.

This is a chapter summarising some of the skills you need at your fingertips to deal with people who make your life hell. If you let others control your life, you may end up looking like a soggy omelette – half-cooked – and that mustn't happen to you. Few will recognise the loneliness, the pain and the uncertainty you are suffering if you don't take control of your life. Your vulnerability may lead you to survive by playing Miss Muffet, Bo-Peep or some other deception if you allow fear to direct your life.

Kelly was just four when she came home from kindergarten proudly carrying her portrait of Humpty Dumpty. Her picture showed the King's men pushing Humpty off the wall. Her older brother objected. 'He fell, stupid! He wasn't pushed!' Kelly looked coolly into his eyes with total certainty. 'Nobody WANTS to jump off high walls,' she said. 'He got pushed!'

There are thousands of ways to maim and murder. Any child watching cartoons can tell you that. Cartoon rocks smash onto the head of countless characters. Victims get up, brush themselves off, and walk away. In real life, your bodies clearly resent physical violence. It is an obvious attempt to break your shell.

Manipulation can produce emotional scars that cut deeply into your shell – they can bleed for a lifetime, threatening your potential as a person. Manipulation is emotional violence. Manipulative wounds may not show, but they never heal. Tragically, these wounds can lead you to injure others.

Emotional violence can be dispensed by a blatant predator, or can slither in softly like a snake, or can cry like a child. These are all strategies to control you. Bullies would have you believe that if you comply, the emotional violence will stop. That's a lie! The demands will never stop. The manipulators feel more powerful in controlling you. They are trying to be safe. They hope you won't notice; they are trying to control your life. Of course you notice. Doing something about it, but not hurting another person, takes skill. These skills are learnable.

We all, even bullies, crave relationships in which we are respected and accepted for the individuals we are. Manipulation mutilates trust. You know you are being bullied.

How do you react to being manipulated? You may cut the relationship dead, leaving a trail of unfinished business. You may choose emotional sterility for protection. Your cowardice is understandable, but you forfeit the one thing that humans crave the most: the joy of being in a relationship where you are loved for who you are, not for what another person wants you to be.

It takes courage to risk relationships when you feel so vulnerable, but safety starts only as you become who you really are. If you spend your energy trying to be somebody else, you won't grow.

Families with the best of intentions frequently demand conformity to old rules that are no longer appropriate. Each of us must walk our own path if we are to reach our potential. Confidence is born of experience, through trusting yourself to take action. When you honour your choices, you are no longer powerless in the face of outside opinion, nor do you have to fight to exist. Confidence is knowing that if you don't like it, you can change it, without hurting someone else. This level of self-esteem only comes with practice.

Kindness, patience, tolerance and appreciation are all acts of love. If you give them to yourself, you will discover that you have everything you need to take you anywhere you want to go. It's wonderful if others approve of you, but that is not what matters. You need the courage to do your own thing, and the intelligence to add to, not mess up, the lives of others.

Learn from everyone, but never try to be someone else. Select the things that will add to your growth as a loving human being, leaving you with the energy to discover the beauty in others.

Needing approval from others can make you vulnerable. You can also make yourself vulnerable carrying on the abuse you've received from others.

What happens when you put yourself down? Self-criticism attacks your potential. You are kicking yourself in the confidence factor. Self-criticism merely identifies something you want to learn or change – be sure the change is not imposed on you by others. When you become your own loving parent, you begin to live. Love who you are, as you are, for with each new second, like the universe, you will be expanding. Honour your courage for trying. Honour what you have achieved and learned. Fear can't occupy a space filled with love.

What happens when you blame others? Blame is a sign of grief and an act of aggression. Revisit to learn, but don't relive a painful experience. In reliving it, you experience the pain as if it were happening all over again. Surely experiencing it once was enough. Look for the gifts. Am I wiser? What am I going to do differently? Seek support, but be careful that the person you choose to support you has a deep commitment to your healing yourself from within. You are all you need.

What do you do if someone blames you? Did they ask, expect or demand what they wanted? Did they consider your needs? Did they suffer in silence expecting you to guess? An expectation is a demand. It is an unjust act. Unresolved issues return like heartburn. Sit down together and fix them! If this person isn't willing to heal the relationship, they don't want it. Write a letter to them, thanking them for the good and bad times. You may never send it, but it will ease the pain and help you learn constructively from the experience. Then move on.

What if you hold back in silence and complain later? You deserve everything others decide to give you! And they will! Take care of yourself, and influence your world. Ask the questions that are soaring through your head. You will be upholding everyone's right to seek information. If you catch yourself saying 'Well, they should know …', make sure they do.

Throw worry in the shredder. Worry is spitting in the eye of life. If you indulge in worry, you'll get what you don't want. Worry is travelling in your imagination. While you are there, work out how you'll handle your worst scenario if it does happen. Then you're ready. Beyond the sun rising and setting, what else comes with a guarantee? Get on with enjoying the beauty of your day.

Are you worried for somebody else? Why are you underestimating their ability to cope and learn from the situation? If you think they are under physical threat, get help. Now!

What if somebody says 'You're wrong!' You are for them, not for you. Criticism is expressing their opinion, not yours.

The cruellest form of this accusation is silent blaming. Some people make sure you know something's wrong by hanging around looking sad. When you ask them, 'What's wrong?' they say, 'Nothing' or 'I told you. You didn't listen'. This sort of person has a greater investment in punishing you than in building the relationship. Love and respect make sure that the message gets through, however long it takes.

Criticism may also be an act of generosity. Consider its possible use.

Sarcasm is a forty-four magnum hiding under a coat of humour. Never defend your right to choose yours, theirs, or anybody else's opinion.

Cynicism? It's the voice of despair from someone doing nothing. They throw acid on ideas, and you'll need to ask them for a contribution. Cynics are too terrified to act. Give them success by noting what they like to do, then ask them to contribute. If they refuse, move on, don't coax! But remember, if they discount contributions, keep asking for their solutions. There is no such thing as a free lunch.

See shame as a wrong turn from which you can learn. There are times when any one of us can act in a way that is alien to the way we want to live. Compassion begins within. Feel the shame, learn from it. How did you get to the level of anger, frustration or envy that got you into that predicament? What are you going to do differently? Heal yourself. Weeds are much easier to deal with when they are small. So are negative feelings.

It is rarely necessary to justify. Justification is an attempt to clarify your actions to someone questioning your choices. The criticism is especially painful when it comes from someone you love, yet when you justify your actions, you are acknowledging their right to question those choices. Accept the gift of their information but always reserve your right of choice. If you work for them, fine. They have a right to that information, but they do not have the right to bully you in the process.

Competition is a war. It's encouraged by our culture. Great if you win, hell if you lose. The pain of losing only occurs if you hang your self-worth onto beating another person. It is opting

for the most violent ride of your life. Compete with yourself –
it's called growth.

Why would you compare? We are not the same, and you might
end up feeling superior or inferior. You are neither. Just glori-
ously different. Comparisons such as 'better than', 'more than'
and 'less than' are competitive, and deserve the shredder. Enjoy
the abundance around you, and within you. It is there.

Others may ask you to choose 'either/or'. Say you want 'all of
the above'! Try that in a restaurant. You'll be surprised how
often you'll get it.

Being perfect means you have nothing left to learn.
Perfectionism is an attempt to reach the 'Safety Zone of Public
Approval'. There is no such place! Insist on using the 'right'
screw to hold up a bridge, but remember that tomorrow that
screw could be obsolete. You are in the business of learning. Can
checking and rechecking add value? If so, do it. If not, decide
how long you are going to fly in a holding pattern burning
valuable resources, then spend a guilt-free day loving your life.
Choose every morning to be happy or anxious. It can change
your life.

'Should'! A very demanding word! Of course you 'should' stop
at red lights, rather than consider them an inconvenience. You
'should' respond positively and constructively in a relationship
or work situation. Question other people's 'shoulds' – they are
often forms of abuse. Do you really want to? Is it adding value
to you and others? Is someone trying to grab your life? Is it a
message from long ago, and no longer appropriate? Once
manipulators smell cracked egg, they are harder to stop. A
healthy relationship does not expect the other person to go belly
up, or fight. If they are not considering your needs as well as
their own, there is no equality.

Conflict offers you a chance to achieve harmony, tranquillity,

balance and, probably, better solutions. Our difference is a powerful database to draw from. An argument is war. As the Master
Tao said: 'The way to win a war is never fire a shot'. Bring the
conflict away from the past by asking 'How do we fix it?'
Otherwise, it gets bogged in perceptions – yours and theirs. Be
first to explore the other's suggestions. Offer yours and make a
commitment to go further than either of you imagined. Co-operation is not soft. It's strength. You are offering commitment,
co-operation and respect. It's stress-free and profitable. Rules,
created together to serve each of you, will hold.

**Has everyone involved made a commitment to be responsible
for the growth of the relationship?** Daring to love, without guarantee of return, is one of the bravest acts you can perform. But
remaining in a relationship where there is no stated, open
commitment on both sides, with evidence to back it up, is a
death wish.

It isn't a relationship if only one person takes responsibility
for its health. It's an empty shell of expectation of hope. Even
massive love on the part of one cannot dint the armour of emotional sterility where intimacy is fraud. Only Samson could hold
the temple up by himself, and not for long.

Love, understanding, support and tolerance are needed most
on bad days, which we all have. The warmth of silence is a
remarkable act of love. 'Want to talk about it? 'Can I help?'
When you tell your partner you need time out, it is not rejection,
unless it's habit-forming, but you must say you need to work
something out on your own and you'll ask for help if you need it.

Smothering your own needs in a relationship is like body surf-
ing in rapids. It is martyrdom, and is both self-abuse and abusive
to others. You will always blame somebody if you choose martyrdom. Discounting another person's opinions and feelings is
abusive. There is no respect. There is always a pay day if you are

abused. The abuser gets it. Or you dump it on yourself or some-one else.

> Over a two-year period, Martin and Andrea, who both worked full time, had ten sessions with a marriage counsellor. Andrea was asking for shared responsibilities at home because she was carrying all the workload of two jobs. She felt in her heart that this was the only way that Martin would learn the justice of shared responsibility for working couples. Martin dismissed her requests, even in written form. Martin said he didn't have a problem, Andrea was just disorganised. At the end of the two years, Andrea departed and left him the children. He was devastated. 'She never gave me any indication she was unhappy!' However, Andrea's action backfired on her. Martin took another partner almost immediately and Andrea was on the outside. Her children felt she had abandoned them. Martin treated his new partner, a professional woman, exactly the same. She left too.

When the other person is unwilling to commit to the growth of the relationship, you aren't friends. When negativity is the norm, there is no justice. Justice begins the moment you stop accepting abuse.

You honour your partner when you accept that they are the ones who must choose their path, and how they want to walk it. You honour yourself when you do the same. We honour each other when we ask 'How's it going?'

The more you develop inner strength, the more you draw healthy people to you. You are the only one who can listen to your inner wisdom. Following it develops confidence. Look at how your ideas can happen. Negative thoughts define the parts of the problem you need to deal with. The act of trying an idea out becomes knowledge. Acknowledging what you liked, what you learned, and what you are going to do next, is living joyously. You deserve it.

Manipulators avoid those with confidence unless they want to be stopped. They know they won't get away with it more than once. If bullies still need to intimidate, they prefer to pick on vulnerable people. The more you value yourself, the easier it will be to see through the masks of fear manipulators wear, to recognise the beauty within in every one of us.

When Holly was a kid, she was called 'stupid'. She wrote backwards. Later, they called her 'dyslexic', but the old scars still bled. In the schoolyard, the other children picked up the chant: 'Stupid, Stupid, Stupid!' Holly wished she was invisible.

In grade five, she had a teacher who had been taught that humiliation was an essential tool to get kids to learn. Holly was humiliated a lot because her teacher always knew when Holly didn't know something. Holly thought Miss Edwards could see inside children's minds, and was very intimidated.

Holly felt alone in the world until an equally stupid boy joined her class. It lightened her humiliation load by 50 per cent. She took great comfort that she wasn't the only freak in the world. It gave her time to explore the art of victimisation.

Whenever Danny was being ridiculed, Holly watched. She noticed that when he was insecure about an answer, he would drop something under his desk. As he reached the object, the teacher would scream his name. Danny would rise slowly to his feet, as if he were going to the gallows. His answer was always wrong.

All the kids knew what happened next. The teacher unleashed her performance. Miss Edwards informed the world that Danny starred in stupidity because he didn't work hard at remembering the right answers. While she debased him, her eyes roamed around the room to judge her impact. Those who worked hard at memory and regurgitation smirked. The rest were suitably cowed, eyes downcast.

It was a system that had forgotten its job was to develop the wonderful potential within each child. There was also a belief that 'bright' children complied. The measurement of success was uniformity and compliance. A gold star indicated you had given the teacher's idea of the right answer. Nobody assumed that children could or should learn to reason and solve problems.

Watching that teacher demolish Danny was an incredible gift for Holly. She created her own safety. When she was confident in her knowledge, she dropped her pen to the floor. She was not disappointed. At the screech of her name, Holly rose to her feet looking suitably downcast, and gave the right answer.

The first time Holly did it, it was her moment of triumph! Miss Edwards was paralysed. It was as if she was on Broadway, and had forgotten her lines. The embarrassed silence seemed to go on forever, and Holly loved every second of the impasse. Of course she couldn't display that.

Previously, whenever Holly thought she had the right answer, she would sit on the edge of her chair, throwing her raised arm out of joint, praying 'Please God, let her ask me. Let me be right for once.' Holly never got her place in the sun. She was told curtly by Miss Edwards, 'Sit down, I know you know'.

Holly was never victimised again. Her hand waved frantically when she didn't know. She dropped something when she did. Miss Edwards felt successful because a lazy child had begun to learn. Holly had learned that manipulation is a survival kit, and if you are smart, it had better be a big kit!

Holly paid a heavy price using manipulation for protection. She was forty-two before she discovered that she was not stupid. It was when she began to discover the person she was, lying dormant, inside. She began to look fear in the eye. As her confidence grew, her major discovery was that the world wasn't so scary after all.

And Danny? He hanged himself when he was seventeen. Holly never forgot it.

YOUR LIFE IS YOURS –
A PRECIOUS GIFT TO HOLD AND UNFOLD.
EVERYTHING YOU NEED YOU HAVE,
AND IT'S WAITING TO BE USED.
NEVER RUN OUT OF JOY.

Appreciation

It is a great privilege to be able to acknowledge the people who have touched my life: the good, the disappointing, the scary and the downright painful – a normal life! They have provided my necessary life experiences and I have tried to learn from them all. Perhaps the disappointments and the painful experiences have had the greatest impact, as their gifts of learning took me longer to spot – embarrassment, anger and self-righteousness got in my way. I found I could only crawl my way back to equilibrium when I had absorbed their lessons.

I have had wonderful support along the way. Al Haggar, a creative generous giant, pestered me for fifteen years to write this book. I felt I needed to understand, to learn a lot more, before I could. Even a few days before he died, Al was coaching me on how to keep it straight and simple. When I was looking for a character to represent the long-term effect of bullying on a person's life, it was Mary Haggar who shouted 'Humpty Dumpty'. I am indebted to them both.

Wilson Main's belief in the need for the book and his open and generous heart were invaluable. He marched me around the world to meet his network and was always there to say 'That works. That doesn't.'

Douglas Flynn supported me without even reading the manuscript, and that was a generous act of faith.

I have had the support of so many friends, my personal Tin Soldiers: Jenny and Rod Davies, Peter and Carol Crossley, Barbara Hughes, and Maggie and Hamish McDonell didn't mind how many times I asked them to listen. Rosemary Oxer kept saying 'Write it as you say it', and James and Alison Grant read every chapter to see if I had. Bob Lallamont could always be counted on for creative input.

I've spent most of my professional life trying to teach managers to be leaders and to recognise that people's individual development and commitment to contribute to others is what produces profitability in organisations. I've learned from great leaders: Peter Fitchett, Jesse Moore and Craig Hunt produce communities in companies by realising the talent of every person who works with them and seeing that their people receive the opportunities that will stretch them. These managers didn't downsize – they upsized, producing teams that value each other, creating ideas and solutions together, proof that a co-operative environment really works.

I must acknowledge human relations practitioners Bruce Rowe, Susan Tonks, James Harper and Therese Warman, who see themselves as internal consultants and know no barriers, from the boardroom to the shop floor.

Joan Woffinden and Elaine Forde were inspirational in founding 'Women in Management', teaching women in the workforce to be responsible for their careers, to not fall into the aggression trap and die early, and to never believe in glass ceilings.

Pathfinders Donald Bartram, David and Pam Mitchell, and Grant Duncan taught me a lot about how they create a holistic medical practice with a single focus - 'Don't get sick', a remarkable example of holding people to be accountable for their health.

I have been blessed with the spiritual wisdom of Bonnie Mathes, Louie Muscara, Jean Hook, Cherie Sutherland and Ann Harrison, who were always there when I thought I'd hit an insurmountable object. Much of their wisdom I've passed on to you.

The substance of David Fox, Greg May and Robert Pullan were always behind me, and I would like to thank them for smoothing the technical paths.

Tony Webster helps kids climb down from scary heights in trees and mountains (see 'Baa Baa Black Sheep' chapter!).

Clare Wallis, as senior editor, has had an incredible ability to listen, translate and make sure you know what I am saying and Megan Johnston helped to clarify an early draft. Brigitta Doyle, thanks for having a hell of a day or we might never come up with your wonderful title.

Most importantly, thank you God for Julie Stanton of Simon and Schuster, who jumped into my head and understood what I was trying to accomplish: 'At the very worst, people will know they aren't suffering alone. At the very best, bullies may discover they are the bully and do something constructive about it, and in-between, the rest of us are going to handle bullies without creating a war.' If you find this book useful you can add your thanks to Julie for her compassion for those who suffer from bullying and her unwavering ability to believe that we can all learn.

I am so grateful for the love I have received from Margie and Mac Yates, and Zib and Bill Wegenast, which has followed me all around the world all my adult life. Their support never wavers.

Lastly, thanks to all of you who have trusted me to help you help yourself. Although the world will never know your names, this book is a summary of your journey, passed on to help those who are still experiencing similar pain. Dear former bullies, thank you for proving conclusively that we are all in the business of discovering who we are. We are all growing.

LOIS GRANT
AUGUST 2001

Lois Grant is a management consultant and counsellor with more than twenty-five years' experience in Australia, New Zealand and the UK.

A former lecturer in communication at the University of South Australia, Lois has worked extensively with many major Australian and international organisations, helping them become 'cooperative communities' rather than 'detached feudal systems'. She has produced eleven videotapes on management topics dealing with human relations, which are being sold in thirty-one countries around the world.

In her counselling practice, Lois has worked extensively with families as well as individuals, and is all too familiar with the destruction that manipulation can produce.

Born in Canada, Lois raised four children in such diverse cultures as Africa, Brazil and Fiji. She has even waltzed with Idi Amin. Idi was the bear who eats Algy! (See page 14.)

Lois has an honours degree in communication from Flinders University, South Australia, and did a post-graduate Master's qualifying study in social psychology at the University of Adelaide. She also has a diploma in Communication from the Academy of Radio Arts, Toronto.

Lois lives in Adelaide, where she continues her consulting and counselling work.